CONDUCTING A COMMUNICATION AUDIT

Promoting Organizational Effectiveness Through Communication Efficiency

CONDUCTING A COMMUNICATION AUDIT

Promoting Organizational Effectiveness Through Communication Efficiency

Michael G. Strawser

University of Central Florida

cognella®

SAN DIEGO

Bassim Hamadeh, CEO and Publisher

Todd R. Armstrong, Publisher

Anne Jones, Project Editor

Jordan Krikorian, Editorial Assistant

Alia Bales, Associate Production Manager

Jess Estrella, Senior Graphic Designer

Trey Soto, Licensing Specialist

Natalie Piccotti, Director of Marketing

Kassie Graves, Senior Vice President, Editorial

Jamie Giganti, Director of Academic Publishing

cognella | ACADEMIC PUBLISHING

3970 Sorrento Valley Blvd., Ste. 500, San Diego, CA 92121

BRIEF CONTENTS ————————

DETAILED CONTENTS ───────

PART II   THE COMMUNICATION AUDIT PROCESS

PREFACE ————————————————

I am a problem solver. I am a college communication professor by day, and although I consistently say that I have my dream job, I also love being out in the community helping organizations understand how to solve their complex challenges. I started my own consulting and training firm, Legacy Communication Training and Consulting, LLC, in order to be more accessible to businesses. What does all of this have to do with a book about communication audits?

In my work, I often find that most business problems are in essence communication problems. The issue is rarely that an organization is not making enough money; instead, it is usually that a relationship or message has broken down throughout the business process. When I consult, I typically find that my clients want help solving communication problems. So I wrote this book about communication audits to help organizations overcome their own communication issues.

The word "audit" probably sounds negative, but for the purposes of this book, it means assessment. In order to successfully solve communication problems, one needs to know how to assess (identify) them. This handbook will help you (1) learn how to diagnose communication problems in organizations and (2) apply this diagnostic information to then enhance communication across the organization.

This text was strategically written to be applicable for different audiences. Students taking business or communication courses will find this information valuable as they try to become more marketable in an increasingly competitive job market. From a content perspective, this book approaches communication audits as data-driven opportunities for applied research, which means that within its pages are components related to data collection and analysis. Therefore, I believe that working professionals in any organization will also find the information within these pages insightful and useful. The tone of the book is intended to be conversational and practical, and the mission of this book is to put communication assessment tools into the hands of anyone and everyone who is willing to help solve communication problems.

Features and Benefits

This book is distinctive in several ways. First, the tone is accessible and approachable. I have tried to write this book as though we are having an informal conversation about organizational communication challenges. Second, the approach I take throughout this book is both academic and personal, meaning I am relying on years of consulting experience as well as research-driven solutions that have been tested and are deemed reliable. Third, the book is meant to be relevant to a world that has succumbed to remote and virtual work while still being applicable to more traditional practices. Fourth, the book is meant to be helpful, so there are activities, tools, and usable resources included in every chapter. Fifth, this book has been designed for all audiences but has been strategically developed as a resource for instructional use.

Organization and Suggestions for Use

This book includes 15 chapters divided into three parts, with professional vignettes from trusted voices who are working in corporate contexts. Part I (Chapters 1–5) provides context for communication in organizations as well as foundational determinations for beginning the audit process. For example, in Chapter 1 we discuss what a communication audit is and the reason(s) why it is important. Then each subsequent chapter covers a different audit component:

- Chapter 2: Communication Consulting in Context

- Chapter 3: Communication *Is* the Organization

- Chapter 4: Determining the Procedure

- Chapter 5: Involving Stakeholders

Part II focuses on the steps involved in a communication audit:

- Chapter 6: The Process, Step 1:
  Needs Assessment

- Chapter 7: The Process, Step 2:
  Collecting Data and Methodology

- Chapter 8: The Process, Step 3:
  Analyzing Data and Clarifying Results

- Chapter 9: The Process, Step 4:
  Communicating the Results

Part III focuses on the practical application as the audit is manifested as a springboard to true organization-wide solutions:

- Chapter 10: Dealing With Results

- Chapter 11: Internal Communication Strategy

- Chapter 12: Infusing an Audit Into Organizational Culture

- Chapter 13: Using Results to Inform Organizational Training

- Chapter 14: External Communication Audits in a Digital World

The last chapter of the book, Chapter 15, provides key chapter summaries as well as the main takeaways for each chapter.

I am a teacher by trade who received my PhD from the University of Kentucky in something called Instructional Communication. I research and write about communication in and through all educational contexts. Because of this, teaching and training are always at the forefront of my mind. My favorite part of my professorial role is engaging and interacting with my students. Because of this, I have created a text that is student-friendly. There is not a lot of jargon, there are embedded activities and discussion questions all throughout, and the work has been structured to be digestible within a standard 15-week class. If I was using this book as a resource in my classes, I would, very simply, start at Chapter 1 and move throughout the content. With that said, the content, activities, and discussion questions can be useful in a corporate context.

Acknowledgments

This book is a product of many years of education, training, and consulting experience. I extend special gratitude to the three scholars who generously reviewed my manuscript draft and whose feedback, suggestions, and encouragement truly helped me make this a better book: Dr. Shawn Apostel (Bellarmine University), Dr. Brian K. Richardson (University of North Texas), and Dr. Roth Smith (Illinois State University). Your collective insight and suggestions have elevated this product and encouraged me to think even more deeply about the text. Finally, I want to thank the entire Cognella team, especially Todd Armstrong. Todd's encouragement and willingness to allow me to be entrepreneurial and creative (as well as autonomous) were a great benefit throughout this process.

PART I

Foundations

CHAPTER 1

What Is a Communication Audit, and Why Is It Important?

This chapter will address communication confusion and communication breakdown, present an overview of communication audits, and connect communication audits to a purposeful communication strategy.

Communication audits are assessment tools that provide an objective look at communication problems and processes within the organization. In most cases, audits have more than one purpose. An audit can be both evaluative and formative. In doing so, it provides an overview of where the organization currently is and offers areas of potential improvement. Communication audits are primarily used as an evaluation tool, though, revealing potential issues. Whether you are measuring communication capacity or performance, an audit can be used to measure effectiveness. But the audit has a method, and the evaluation has a procedure. It is important that the appropriate steps are followed. And by following the steps outlined in this handbook, you can save yourself money by conducting the audit internally instead of hiring an outside consultant. Or, if you are a student who wants to prove your ultimate value and worth to a company, you can add the communication audit as yet one more tool in your professional toolbox.

Communication issues happen all the time. On a personal level, think about your last holiday. While discussing politics, sports, or the stock market, did someone make an assertion that was interpreted incorrectly? On a professional level, have you ever misdiagnosed an issue or had a conflict with a colleague at work? We experience communication misunderstandings consistently throughout our day. Sometimes, these are internal moments of confusion, but often, our confusion occurs because of various factors. Communication audits help us think about communication effectiveness first at the individual level and then at the corporate or institutional level. This chapter will address communication confusion and will paint a clear picture of why your organization should conduct a communication audit to address confusing or ineffective communication.

Communication Confusion

George Bernard Shaw, the famed playwright, is credited with saying that the single biggest problem in communication is the illusion that it has taken place. In other words, we assume that the transfer of information leads to automatic understanding by the audience, and that just is not the case. Instead, we often try to add more information to our message, which can cause even more confusion! The cycle continues on forever in some cases.

The traditional model of communication (Source → [Message] → Receiver) is still valuable for our world today, but new channels, mediums, and media have complicated how we transfer information and even how we process information. Despite these issues, significant opportunity exists. Our communication capabilities are unparalleled, and never before has information been so accessible. As we continue to consider how we can use all of our societal communication powers for good, it's important to remember that communication is

- a process, not a thing;
- circular, not linear;
- complex;
- irreversible; and
- involves the total personality.

Once we accept these ideas—that communication is a process that is interactive, complex, irreversible, and holistic—we can strive for effectiveness. Access to information is easy and expedient (for most), but the purposeful utilization and communication of that information is neither easy nor expedient. Communication is *not* easy. There are communication barriers and challenges we have to deal with all the time, including distractions, noise, incorrect information, inefficient deliver—the list is seemingly endless. We create messages to persuade, contradict, confuse, overload, and overwhelm. But we need to continue to think about communication as a mechanism to build continuous improvement, develop accountability, make optimal decisions, allocate resources, build relationships, achieve true understanding, and gain insight. Communication audits can help organizations solve complex communication issues. A communication audit helps answer the following:

- What questions are you, the communicator, trying to ask and answer?

- Why are you asking or answering certain questions?

- Why do you need to communicate this message?

- What are you trying to improve?

- Is your message credible and consistent?

- Will your message inspire change?

Generally, a communication audit helps us avoid communication confusion and readjust when communication breakdown occurs. Ideally, we would be so effective at communicating that we wouldn't need to audit or assess our communication strategy. But that is not realistic. As we move along this process of trying to communicate our message, breakdowns and confusion are bound to occur.

Communication Breakdown

A communication breakdown can happen for a variety of reasons, and next we will cover some of the main culprits.

INADEQUATE INFORMATION

Sometimes information is, genuinely, inadequate—meaning we don't have enough of the information to make a legitimate decision. This happens in cases where we are awaiting further clarification or waiting on additional data. In cases like this, it is important to highlight which data remains untapped or unknown. Without adequate information, we cannot ask the right questions, follow the correct processes or procedures, or even take the next step in a decision-making process.

Questions to Consider

1. Do you find that you often lack relevant information?

2. Is your decision making stalled because you don't know the answers to all your questions?

3. Are your employees requesting additional information that you don't have right now?

INFORMATION OVERLOAD

The idea of information overload probably rings true for many of us; after all, we are living in what has been called the Information Age. The tendency is to think that a communication problem (or, to be honest, most problems in general) can be solved with more information, but this often leads to information overload. It is also easy to want to communicate more, and more often, considering the accessibility and availability of so many communication tools. However, the result is a combustible volcano of information that never stops. Unfortunately, information overload can be paralyzing, frustrating, and, generally, not helpful.

Questions to Consider

1. Is your tendency to send additional memos, emails, or information when something does not go according to plan?

2. Do you feel compelled to include all information in one source or document?

3. Do you believe more information is always better?

POOR-QUALITY INFORMATION

Unlike inadequate information, poor-quality information is more an issue of reliability and validity. If you are experiencing issues resulting from poor-quality information, like poor message clarity, that means you are potentially receiving information that is not accurate (i.e., wrong) instead of inadequate (i.e., not enough). Poor-quality information impacts the process, as decisions may need to be remade to deal with misinformation. In some ways, poor-quality information has a substantial effect on morale as well.

Questions to Consider

1. Do you request and receive information from credible sources?

2. Have you double-checked crucial or mission-critical information?

3. Are your information sources regularly incorrect or inaccurate?

POOR TIMING

Sometimes, communication is accurate and appropriate but mistimed. A memo to the team during a budget crisis about salary reductions for midlevel managers while C-suite executives receive a raise would be a poorly timed message (you may laugh, but it happens more than you would think). Another example of a poorly timed message could be a risk warning sent to stakeholders too late. Poor timing can also be contextual and may lead to mismanaged deadlines. There may be governmental, cultural, or societal influences that have made your message inappropriate or in poor taste.

Questions to Consider

1. Have you considered the optics of your information transfer?

2. Is there anything external (or internal) that would affect the delivery of this message?

3. If you want to deliver this message, who is most impacted?

4. Is your information urgent?

LACK OF FEEDBACK OR FOLLOW-UP

A communication breakdown may occur because the message receiver did not reciprocate a desired response or may not have provided any response at all. This can cause the sender to assume the message has been misunderstood or missed altogether. A lack of feedback or inadequate follow-up has ramifications for process and procedure, project outcomes and deliverables, and workplace relationships. In addition, we may have a tendency to assume that when we do not hear from someone, they have received the message, read it, and understood it *as we intended*. The follow-up communication is then built on false assumptions.

Questions to Consider

1. Have you provided opportunities for people to provide feedback?
2. Do you have a follow-up plan after you communicate the intended message?
3. Do people have action items or know how feedback/follow-up will be achieved?

PROBLEMS WITH CHANNELS

Communication channels are the actual modality or method you use to transfer messages. For example, email is probably one of your primary channels. In addition, social media, email blasts, complaint channels, and so on may all be popular platforms. Breakdowns because of channel issues can range from something happening to the technology (maybe a lack of bandwidth) to something occurring within the actual message itself (e.g., a social media post is tone-deaf). The generation gap and certain generational tendencies related to communication channel preference may also illuminate channel-based challenges. Needless to say, an audit cannot solve communication issues without taking into consideration the methods and platforms that are actually used to communicate.

Questions to Consider

1. Can the desired end result of your message be achieved through this channel?

2. What interpretations or assumptions are tied to this channel?

3. What industry standards are most effective for using this channel?

INEFFECTIVE GOAL SETTING

There are instances when communication incompetence has occurred because the foundation is broken. The foundation in this context is the goal that the communication is trying to achieve. A mismanaged goal results in communication that has missed the mark, which usually leads to an undesirable end result. Ineffective goal setting, then, is just as much an issue of process and unclear expectations. Communication would, obviously, be negatively impacted if you were aiming for the wrong goal.

Questions to Consider

1. Has a strategic plan been presented that gives a communication directive?

2. Has the strategic plan received approval from proper channels?

3. Have you identified how the communication strategy connects to the goal?

COMMUNICATION ANXIETY

Communication anxiety is not just limited to public speaking classes and can significantly impact corporate communication. Research tells us that many struggle with varying levels of anxiety related to communication. Feeling anxious about speaking in front of others or communicating interpersonally is not something to be embarrassed by and instead can be an opportunity for growth. Needless to say, anxiety can have implications for communication effectiveness. As a result of communication anxiety, our messaging may be unclear or disjointed because of our inability to control the physical or psychological ramifications of our nerves.

Questions to Consider

1. Are you nervous to share your thoughts or opinions in a group setting?

2. Do you find that your anxiety makes your messages unclear?

CULTURAL BARRIERS

Finally, communication breakdowns can occur, especially in our global marketplace, because of cultural barriers. Not limited to language, although that can be significant, cultural barriers can be difficult to overcome, and as a result, communication may suffer. Cultural barriers may include explicit or implicit verbal messages, how close people are physically, the use of nonverbal elements (e.g., gestures, facial expressions, vocal tone, etc.), or even eye movements and eye contact. These cultural barriers can lead to substantial misunderstandings.

Questions to Consider

1. Does your organization struggle to understand how to communicate to different cultural audiences?

2. Do the messages from your organization seem to ignore cultural distinctions?

3. Does a lack of cultural competence impact your internal organizational relationships?

Communication breakdowns happen all the time in our personal relationships and in our professional work environments. It is important that we identify where misunderstanding and ineffective communication occurs in order to establish a way forward to achieve mutual understanding and communication competence.

TABLE 1.1   Communication Breakdowns

Inadequate information	There is not enough information to make a decision.
Information overload	The amount and depth of information have caused decision paralysis.
Poor-quality information	The information presented is not accurate.
Poor timing	The timing of the communication was, or may be, ill-timed.
Lack of feedback or follow-up	A response from the receiver is either not solicited or not offered.
Problems with channels	The actual method or medium used to transport the message is not effective.
Ineffective goal setting	The foundational goals have been misappropriated or mismanaged.
Communication anxiety	Nerves or anxiety toward an individual or situation cause disjointed or unclear communication.
Cultural barriers	Cultural differences impact information transfer and mutual understanding.

Communication Audit:
What Does It Accomplish?

QUESTION

In your own words, what can a communication audit accomplish?

_____

_____

_____

_____

_____

_____

The communication breakdowns mentioned above can be targeted, identified, and solved with an effective communication audit. Again, an audit is an objective look at communication problems and processes within the organization. This objective look should lead to determining whether or not communication activities within an organization are effective and efficient. An audit answers whether or not an organization's communication process and messaging works. Ultimately, communication audits do just what the name implies: They take an overarching audit of the communication practices of an organization to determine if the communication practices are effective. Typically, audits involve an assessment of internal communication, but clients and other external stakeholders can also be involved. The audit help assess when individuals are getting too much or too little information.

Benefits of Communication Audits

A communication audit is useful in multiple ways. For one, it helps organizations determine communication strengths and weaknesses. Clarity of messaging, both internal and external, can also be evaluated. If your goal is external, an audit allows you to identify the opinions of your customers and the success of media messaging and/or public relations efforts in a holistic manner. Finally, communication audits help supervisors, managers, and C-suite executives determine if communication efforts are aligned with the mission, vision, and strategic plan of the organization.

Audits can include several moving parts. While most data is collected through connection with team members or clients, an audit can also evaluate policies and procedures, structure, and mediums. A thorough assessment of all communication channels and messaging is, or perhaps should be, an industry standard.

The benefits of a communication audit are seemingly endless. This may sound like a gross generalization, but it really is not. An audit helps you determine action items that can help you improve your overall communication strategy. Making sure all communication efforts in your organization are aligned and effective can help your people to feel less overwhelmed and your customers better understand your brand and mission.

So, why conduct a communication audit? See Figure 1.1 for an overview of the various reasons.

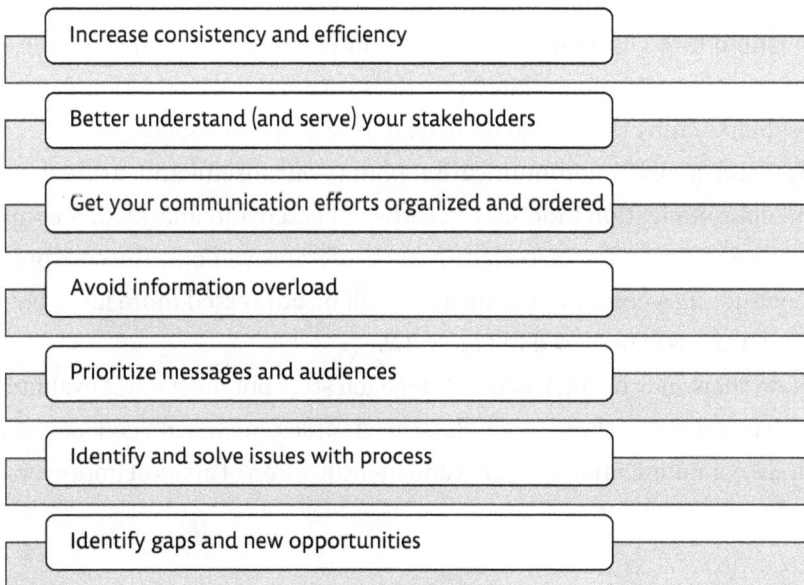

- Increase consistency and efficiency
- Better understand (and serve) your stakeholders
- Get your communication efforts organized and ordered
- Avoid information overload
- Prioritize messages and audiences
- Identify and solve issues with process
- Identify gaps and new opportunities

| Figure 1.1 Reasons to Conduct a Communication Audit

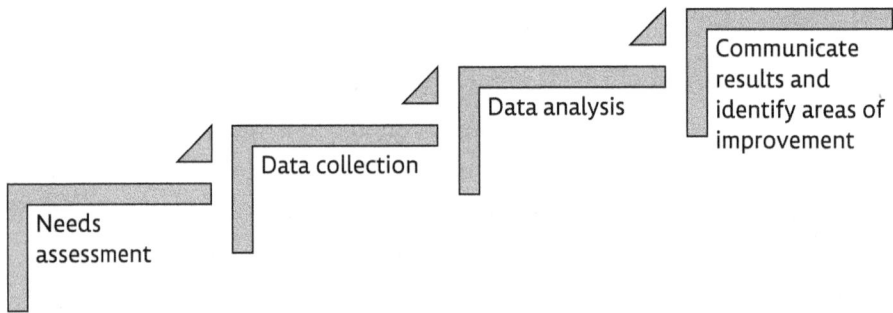

| Figure 1.2 General Communication Audit Process

Ultimately, a communication audit is performed to align communication efforts to the organization's strategic efforts. As such, it will help you identify and assess current communication goals and objectives; gaps or issues with the current communication plan (assuming you have one; if not, an audit can help you design and develop a strategic communication plan); clarity and consistency of messages; audience engagement; and overall communication effectiveness. More information is not the answer. We need *targeted* communication efforts.

A purposeful communication plan can be developed once an audit is completed and will usually emphasize strategy, implementation, and support. Those who are communicating and, ultimately, those who are assessing communication efforts should identify the core tasks of a communication effort, understand how communication will be implemented, and be familiar with any non-communication-related practices within the organization that could either help or hurt the end goal associated with the message.

To determine if a communication plan is purposeful and strategic, data about communication practices must be collected and analyzed. A communication audit will then help identify areas of improvement. The core process for conducting a communication audit will be addressed more later, but the general process is reviewed in Figure 1.2.

Now, there may be intricacies under each step, but most audit evaluations will fall under one of these core pillars: needs assessment; data collection; data analysis; communication of results and identification of areas of improvement.

Building a Communication Strategy Through a Communication Audit

A communication audit can help you establish a purposeful and data-driven communication strategy. This strategy will, hopefully, address effectiveness as it relates to the audience, perceptions, purpose of the message, data/information available, and the end result. Figure 1.3 highlights categories to consider as you build a purposeful communication strategy. Ultimately, an audit can help you think about each category and identify channels to effectively communicate your message either internally or externally.

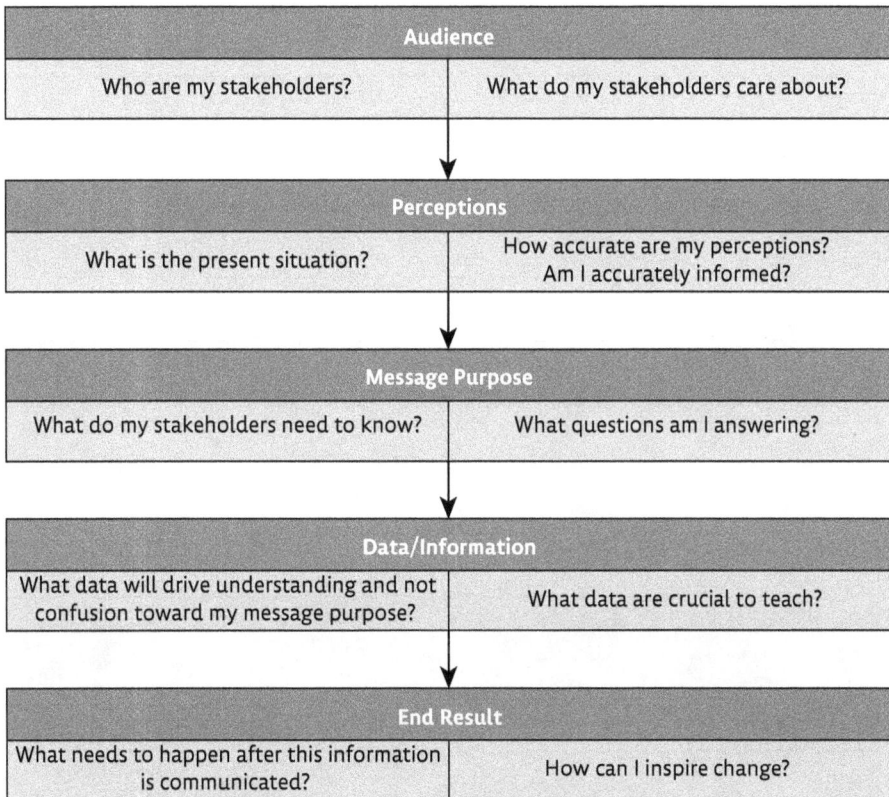

Audience	
Who are my stakeholders?	What do my stakeholders care about?

Perceptions	
What is the present situation?	How accurate are my perceptions? Am I accurately informed?

Message Purpose	
What do my stakeholders need to know?	What questions am I answering?

Data/Information	
What data will drive understanding and not confusion toward my message purpose?	What data are crucial to teach?

End Result	
What needs to happen after this information is communicated?	How can I inspire change?

| Figure 1.3 Purposeful Communication Strategy

The remainder of this book explores how to conduct a communication audit and how to use the results of an audit to change your organization. Communication *is* the organization. Your messages, both internally and externally, should be intentionally crafted to ensure maximum impact.

ACTIVITIES AND DISCUSSION QUESTIONS

1. What organizational communication issues do you think are more pressing/challenging? What organizational communication issues do you think are more common? Why?

    _____

    _____

    _____

    _____

    _____

    _____

2. What does effective communication in organizations entail?

    _____

    _____

    _____

    _____

    _____

    _____

3. What are some benefits of an effective communication strategy?

    _____

    _____

    _____

    _____

_____

_____

WHAT WOULD YOU DO?

Imagine you are an influential leader in an organization with substantial communication challenges. How would you convince others in the organization to analyze internal communication by completing a communication audit? What arguments would you use to support the audit's implementation? How would you articulate the communication challenges facing the organization?

_____

_____

_____

_____

_____

_____

_____

_____

_____

CHAPTER 2

Communication Consulting in Context

This chapter will discuss communication consulting as a viable career option, address internal communication consultation as a role of the communication specialist, and connect communication audits to communication consulting.

It may seem odd to start with a communication audit overview and then move immediately into a discussion about communication consulting, but if you think about it, the transition is understandable. When you conduct a communication audit for an organization, either as an inside or outside voice, you are serving as a consultant. Specifically, you are trying to help the organization solve a known (or, more likely, unknown) communication problem. As such, you are trying to gather data to help demonstrate that the problem exists and potentially provide information to help the organization solve the problem. To help clarify the consultant's role, this chapter will provide an overview of communication consulting and some helpful tips to the aspiring consultant.

The Role of the Consultant

Everyone wants to be a consultant. Well, probably not everyone, but you understand the sentiment. The consultant's job is desirable. If you are external, you can come into an organization when needed, gather data, and usually leave the organization personally unscathed. Consultants tend to have high price tags—the good ones, at least—and for those with a shortened attention span, the consultant job is great because you can move to new projects quickly. I wanted to become a consultant because I wanted to solve problems. That's why I study communication: I want to solve communication-related problems. Without standing too long on my soapbox, I would like to express that I am concerned with research that is not applied, especially communication research. Practical application of evidence-based research should be a natural inclination, not a rarity. I consult so that I can help apply research to complex corporate communication problems.

I believe the problem-solving mantra is central to how a consultant should function. In fact, Waldeck et al. (2012) believe diagnosing problems is the first and foremost task of the consultant. They focus on three other tasks as well: recommending solutions, facilitating interventions, and evaluating outcomes (see Figure 2.1).

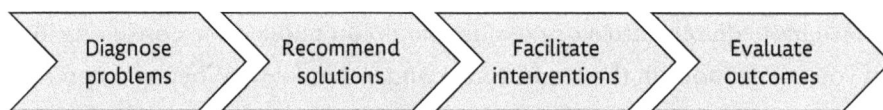

| Diagnose problems | Recommend solutions | Facilitate interventions | Evaluate outcomes |

| Figure 2.1 Communication Consultant Tasks

COMMUNICATION CONSULTANT TASKS

These consulting standards present a wonderful foundation to a conversation: "What can I do, and how can I help?" Working in an organization (any organization) requires problem-solving skills that lead to effective solutions. Properly facilitating interventions (i.e., solving the problem) and evaluating what works are steps that can be accomplished by most competent employees. But sometimes it takes an expert, an outside observer—a consultant.

Diagnose Problems

Leaders (and managers) are usually effective because they are forward thinking. They can see problems before they happen and can implement forward-thinking, strategic solutions. Sometimes, though, you may not know a problem exists (i.e., you don't know what you don't know). Problems can be multifaceted. It may be that your company has survived doing the status quo and have now stagnated. It may be that your organization has lost the core of its mission or vision. It may be that you are spread too thin (as a leader, as an employee, or as an organization). It may be that your employees are lacking the training they need to do a job effectively. There are seemingly endless potential problems.

I like consulting for a lot of reasons, but as I mentioned before, I really enjoy identifying problems and, even more so, solving them. Communication problems can be obvious, but many times communication issues are under the surface. They are bubbling and boiling, just waiting to erupt. Maybe employees are oversaturated with messages and cannot identify key tasks. Or maybe there are personnel issues, where relationships are negative, bitter, and festering. There could be a lack of trust between employees and the supervisor or between peers. These are all communication issues. A consultant can help you diagnose these problems and work toward a solution.

Recommend Solutions

If you are like me, you want to be "quick to solve." In some ways, this is a wonderful trait. The ability to "solve" problems is a fantastic characteristic. People who can solve problems are valuable to any organization. I believe, though, that you cannot solve problems without first diagnosing problems accurately (this is where a communication audit is necessary). To solve problems, you have to first listen to those within the organization. It is easy to walk into a situation, without context, and start telling people what to do, but good consultants listen to those around them and recommend solutions that are tailored to the organization (not just a one-size-fits-all approach). A good communication consultant recommends solutions, absolutely, but a good communication consultant recommends solutions based on listening to, and diagnosing, actual problems.

If you continue to cut off the branches of a tree without ever attacking the root, the branches continue to grow. This is the same with complex organizational problems. A consultant who is worth the organization's time and money will diagnose real problems and provide solutions that achieve holistic change, not just periphery suggestions. But this takes time, takes trust, and takes effort.

Facilitate Interventions

Not all consultants facilitate interventions, but some do. These interventions often occur through corporate training initiatives. Corporate training can be dull, drab, and check-box ready. Here's what I mean: Some organizations are quick to look at training needs and search for the path of least resistance instead of actually searching for training (and a trainer) who can help the organization in both the short and long term. A communication consultant or, in some cases, a communication trainer should facilitate interventions that resonate with the organization's mission and solve the corporation's complex problems or, at the very least, move a potential solution forward. Remember:

- Training does not have to be boring.

- Training does not have to be drab.

- Training does not have to be a waste of time.

- Training does not have to be a "check mark" in an otherwise minimalist development vision.

Instead, I firmly believe that organizational training and professional development, when done well, can enhance a culture and clarify misconceptions. They can help your bottom line, establish a clear mission and vision, and ensure that all employees are on the same page. But, again, training without an evidence-based foundation could be a waste of resources.

Some organizations prefer out-of-the-box or off-the-shelf training. These can be helpful, sure, but wouldn't you rather work with a consultant who has listened to your organizational challenges and crafts a training plan suited around your needs and your people? It is about the organization and the people in the organization. If you want to be a consultant or a communication specialist, focus on solving complex problems, and be willing to put in the work to create outcomes and objectives suited to the needs of the organization.

Evaluate Outcomes

Finally, a consultant can evaluate outcomes. An audit can help with each stage of the process, but it is especially useful here. Once you have established influence and made suggestions for change, the consultant then needs to determine whether or not this change was effective. In this way, then, the consultant evaluates outcomes. We need to determine whether or not something that was suggested and put into action did, in fact, work.

QUESTION

Which consultant role (diagnose, recommend, facilitate, or evaluate) is more appealing to you, and why?

_____

_____

_____

_____

_____

The Consultant as Influencer and Change Agent

If the process above sounds appealing to you, you may want to start considering being a consultant. Consultants exist in almost every industry—and for good reason. An effective and competent consultant can provide significant value for an organization. For context, Peter Block (2011), a well-known consultant and an expert on the actual role of the consultant, defines a *consultant* as a "person in a position to have some influence over an individual, group, or an organization but no direct power to make changes or implement programs" (p. 2). Bellman (1990) says it this way: "Though I see consultants primarily as guides who help clients to use their own resources better, the fact is that we do occasionally have a useful answer or solution" (p. 159). No matter how you define it, consultants can serve both as facilitators and influencers.

Typically, consultants provide information. At times, an organization may allow a consultant to provide direct suggestions, as the above process indicates, or, more specifically, to implement direct suggestions. In most cases, a consultant will collect data and share their interpretation of the data. There is, however, an influence and power that consultants hold. As those responsible for collecting and interpreting data, consultants can set an agenda or a trajectory for an organization. And that power allows the consultant to be a substantial voice for organizational change.

I like Block's definition of "consultant" because it establishes the importance of consultants. Consultants are not castoffs, unimportant participants in a process, or unnecessary expenses. Instead, consultants, who understand how to consult and have a subject matter expertise, can be incredible assets.

Communication consultants are extremely important. Theoretically, an effective communication consultant can pinpoint strategic communication problems and suggest possible solutions. The communication consultant is primarily a communication expert but is also a people expert. They can develop mechanisms to understand where communication breakdowns and confusion occurs. However, Block (2011) highlights a major issue:

> Most problems have a human element in them, and if the prevailing organizational climate is fear, insecurity, or mistrust, people may withhold or distort essential information on the human part of the problem. Without valid data, accurate assessment becomes impossible. (p. 24)

Consultants can help provide a psychologically safe environment where people can freely share their concerns. In this vein, consultants are collaborative problem solvers. They work with an organization to develop solutions to complex problems to then ensure that the problems stay solved. They won't want to provide short-term recommendations for long-term problems.

A consultant, then, must understand systems, structures, and relationships. They must be, simultaneously, agents of change (Czarniawska & Mazza, 2003) and helpers or guides. It is important to remember that the sheer presence of a consultant may spur the organization on to make changes. As such, though, the consultant has significant responsibility. The consultant, whether internal or external, should also be an ethical agent for change, dedicated to leaving the organization better than they found it and determined to do no harm to the organization or their stakeholders. Thankfully, communication audits can help consultants pinpoint where communication issues may exist. By identifying the root cause of communication inefficiency, consultants can provide value to organizations by using their findings to influence output and hopefully improve the bottom line. In this way, audits provide valuable insight into the organization.

THE CONSULTANT AS COMMUNICATOR

Consultants, no matter their subject matter expertise, should be excellent communicators themselves. In fact, von Platen (2015) even refers to communication consultants as "management translators." For our purposes, consultants can use communication audits to more effectively share their findings with their client or audience. In this way, communication audits become both the means to advocate for change in an organization and the platform that consultants use to solidify their position.

Because of their end goal (i.e., to exert influence over complex problems), consultants must be adept at communicating their findings and providing value. The consultant can and should provide input that the organization can use to meet their goals. Communication consultants provide input on how communication can be used to reach those organizational goals more effectively.

THE PROFESSIONAL CONSULTANT

Consultants can achieve their goals in varying professional capacities. With that said, generally they will be either be an external consultant or an internal consultant, in which case they may not even be called a "consultant" but rather a "communication specialist." Internal communication consultants can use communication audits to provide updates on their systemic processes and measure effectiveness. Internally, then, the audit can help internal specialists or consultants communicate their value to their supervisors or establish credibility with their coworkers. External consultants can use communication audits as data or evidence to identify where and why change is needed.

THE INTERNAL CONSULTANT

Internal consultants are unique in their consultancy role. They are organizational change agents. They have great credibility, hopefully, within the organization because of their understanding of the intricate systems present within the organization. In addition, their credibility has usually developed as a result of historical interactions. There is an embedded trust because people know the consultant understands the organization and has its best interests in mind. Unfortunately, though, because they are internal, consultants who work for the organization tend to have the corporation's agenda in mind. This may cause some undue or unneeded conflicts of interest if there are potential competing challenges. Because of this, the internal consultant should have a platform that allows for continuous data collection. Without a clear foundation, suggestions for change will not have the desired effect. Kenton and Moody (2003) believe that one of the significant issues internal consultants face is the ability to truly influence cultural change, as opposed to just initiating new behaviors. If internal consultants want to institute and influence true cultural change, they need a legitimate process that allows them to communicate what is really happening in the organization, not just perpetuate current perceptions or preconceptions. Internal consultants can be extremely important to the growth and success of the organization, but the role has challenges.

THE EXTERNAL CONSULTANT

The external consultant tends to arrive on scene a with a little more gravitas. Most of my consulting endeavors are external. In general, an organization will bring me in as a communication consultant to diagnose or help with some communication issue. In my opinion, most organizational issues are communication related (more on this in Chapter 3). I have worked with organizations because of perceived relational conflict, leadership concerns, issues related to employee retention and talent optimization, and challenges related to information transfer. External consultants usually have an established reputation or credibility and status as an expert. Because of their external nature, consultants outside of the organization have an objectivity that allows them to see organizational issues from a different perspective, with an unbiased opinion. Their objectivity also allows external consultants to have more difficult conversations that the internal consultant may not be able to have, because they are reliant upon the organization for employment and embedded in the fabric of the company.

The Communication Audit: A Necessary Tool for the Communication Consultant

What does all this mean? First, it is important to remember that if you are a subject matter expert, you may start thinking about becoming a consultant. Obviously, other skills are needed beyond subject matter expertise, but having something you know deeply and a subject in which you are considered an expert is a valuable commodity today. While consultants can be subject matter experts in any number of subjects, communication experts are uniquely valuable (we will discuss this more in Chapter 3). The subject matter expertise is important, but consultants need additional tools in their toolkit if they want to provide as much value as possible for an organization. Block (2011) believes that "using valid data eliminates a major cause of confusion, uncertainty, and resulting inefficiency in problem solving. Valid data encompass two things: (1) objective data about ideas, events, or situations that everyone accepts as facts and (2) personal data" (p. 18). This is where the communication audit becomes an important tool for both internal and external consultants.

A communication audit can be the primary tool you use to influence organizational communication-based decisions. It allows for objective data collection and personal data. The audit itself can also be flexible and can fit the organization's needs. The chapters that follow will give you a streamlined process for crafting a communication audit that collects valuable organizational information. Before you move on to Chapter 3, reflect on the following questions as you think about the role of the consultant and navigating organizational dynamics as a communication expert.

ACTIVITIES AND DISCUSSION QUESTIONS

1. In your own words, define the role of the consultant. What do they do? Why are they valuable?

   _____

   _____

   _____

   _____

   _____

   _____

2. Do you think an internal or external communication consultant would be most helpful? Why?

   _____

   _____

   _____

   _____

   _____

   _____

3. Of the four communication consultant tasks mentioned above (diagnose problems, recommend solutions, facilitate interventions, and evaluate outcomes), which do you think is the most important task, and why?

   _____

   _____

_____

_____

_____

_____

4. How can a communication consultant use a communication audit to benefit the organization?

_____

_____

_____

_____

_____

_____

WHAT WOULD YOU DO?

Imagine you are an internal communication specialist. You have noticed that there are significant communication challenges across the organization. Several issues, though, have to do with specific individuals/personnel. How would you approach a communication audit situation where you know there may be personnel recommendations (meaning someone may need to be let go) in a way that is ethical and forthright?

_____

_____

_____

_____

_____

_____

_____

_____

_____

CHAPTER 3

Communication *Is* the Organization

This chapter will explore communication in organizational contexts. What 21st-century methods, modes, and media have changed how and why organizations communicate? In addition, this chapter will provide an overview of how communication has changed for organizations, both internally and externally, and will provide a rationale for assessing communication.

Communication in Organizations

Organizations are never stagnant. They grow, they develop, they become more (and less) effective. But no matter what an organization is responsible for achieving, they consistently and continually change. Organizations are dynamic, living and breathing organisms (Arghode et al., 2020), and this reality should help us consider how the organization functions.

If you like to think about or read about leadership, you should take time to consider how leadership theories have changed over time. McGregor's Theory X and Theory Y dominated the 1960s and situated two different work styles and approaches to work itself. McGregor's (1960) emphasis was on the worker or the individual. The main focus of the 1970s was the SWOT (strengths, weaknesses, opportunities, and threats) analysis, and strategic planning rose to prominence (Stait, 1972). The human factor was still important, but managers assumed all employees could be helped by systemic and strategic changes. In the 1980s, organizations started to take their strategy and develop true and leaner (or more efficient) systems that accomplished more with less and really homed in on process, procedure, and productivity (Krafcik, 1988). In the 1990s, organizations optimized processes, especially through technology. The 2000s brought a renewed emphasis on data, especially big data (Bollier, 2010), and now, in 2020, the human factor and the need for "soft" skills, like communication, is again at the forefront. A timeline of this leadership evolution is included below in Figure 3.1.

QUESTION

Think ahead: What may define the next business generation?

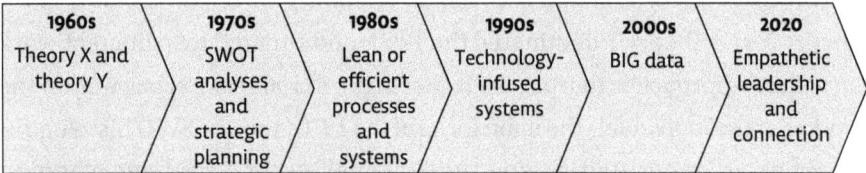

_____

_____

_____

_____

_____

_____

1960s	1970s	1980s	1990s	2000s	2020
Theory X and theory Y	SWOT analyses and strategic planning	Lean or efficient processes and systems	Technology-infused systems	BIG data	Empathetic leadership and connection

| Figure 3.1 Communication Timeline

Here's the reality. There is at least one common theme from the 1960s through today: communication. Whether the organization is people or process oriented, and hopefully the organization is both, communication is needed to achieve organizational goals. Even as more organizations utilize automation, people are still needed, and as such, communication should still be a foundation of the modern organization. If the organization is going to be as effective as possible, it needs to consider communication systems throughout. In many ways, communication *is* the organization, and because communication is not only integral to organizations but is the defining feature of organizations, communication audits have a central place in organizational communication analysis. Without effective communication—both internal, within the organization, and external—to stakeholders and clients, the organization will struggle to be effective and, even more so, may struggle to survive.

Communicating Internally

Generally, internal communication should be the lifeline for increasing effectiveness of an organization. Communication at the internal level can manifest itself in many ways. It can include how a boss or supervisor gives an employee directions or transfers information. It may be how two coworkers approach and address conflict. Internal communication may also be task driven, solely focused on accomplishing varying goals or outcomes. No matter the form or function communication inside the organization takes, we know that internal communication is integral to organizational success (Welch & Jackson, 2007). Thankfully, communication audits can really help improve productivity, reduce absenteeism, create higher quality products and service, increase motivation and innovation, and lower costs (Clampitt & Downs, 1993).

Communication audits can help achieve greater effectiveness in all internal communication domains: business communication (communication skills of employees), management communication (management skills and capabilities for communication), corporate communication (formal communication), and organizational communication (philosophical issues related to the organization's communication). Audits are a helpful mechanism for specifying where an internal communication breakdown has occurred and, maybe more importantly, starting to streamline or begin a conversation about how to improve each domain.

As you can imagine, almost all facets of the organization can be influenced by more effective internal communication. From a big picture perspective, effective internal communication can increase effectiveness as well as employee engagement (Karanges et al., 2015). If employees feel engaged, organizations will generally see a reduced level of turnover (Kang & Sung, 2017). Increased engagement may lead to a more positive organizational culture. What does this all mean? Communication influences everything.

As an assessment tool, communication audits do just what the name implies: They take an overarching audit of the communication practices of an organization to determine if the they are working. Typically, audits do focus on internal communication, but clients and other external stakeholders can also be involved if the organization wants a more external focus. A communication audit is useful in multiple ways. For one, it helps organizations determine communication strengths and weaknesses, thus aiding internal communication. Clarity of messaging can also be evaluated. If your goal is external, an audit allows you to identify the opinions of your customers and the success of media messaging and/or public relations efforts holistically. Finally, communication audits help supervisors, managers, and C-suite executives determine if communication efforts are aligned with the mission, vision, and strategic plan of the organization.

Sources of Communication in Organizations

If you are an active employee of any organization, it may feel like you are overwhelmed and bombarded with information on a regular basis. This information overload element is hard to overcome in part because of the different channels we have to communicate information. Internally, employees receive information through varying channels. The three most popular or common include hierarchical, mass media, and social media/networks. Hierarchical sources include CEOs, presidents, vice presidents, managers, directors, supervisors, and anyone who has a role with authority over others in the organization. Unlike hierarchical sources, mass media sources refer to internal communication that reaches broad audiences (e.g., the entire organization) through mediums like email blasts, newsletters, videos, blogs, and so on. Finally, social media/networks include websites, such as internal portals that are similar to social media websites; social media websites such as LinkedIn and Facebook; and the informal communication networks that exist between employees. The best internal communication strategies use these channels to help maximize the effectiveness of sharing information with employees to further improve communication satisfaction and engagement, which are strongly correlated to employee retention.

ACTIVITY

Where do messages in your organization come from? In the table below, list different hierarchical, mess media, and social media/network channels that influence your organization.

Hierarchical	Mass	Social media/network

Hierarchical communication remains the most traditional method of internal communicating. The different structures we see in our organizations generally have a common or core theme: leader → followers. Because we still see people in authoritative or leadership positions, the hierarchical element continues to be an important and necessary mode of communication. Especially within hierarchical confines, the effectiveness of hierarchical communication often depends on the individual communicator rather than a specific tool or platform. As you can imagine, and probably as you have experienced, super-visors will all have different levels of communication competency.

Thankfully, communication audits allow you to review all levels of the organization and determine where communication breakdowns have occurred. This means you can structure your communication audit to focus on people or individual leaders, structures, mass messages, or social networks.

Assessing Communication Preferences

As you can imagine, members of an organization have varying communication styles and preferences. This reality makes being a leader or a manager extremely difficult. It is absolutely true that you cannot please everyone, especially as it relates to communication. There are many different nuances, and debates rage on about what exactly constitutes a true communication preference. For example, how do employees prefer to handle conflict? Do they like to avoid the issue or address it head on? A preference can also be related to how someone receives information. Do they like a lot of details or minimal details and no interference? The other complicating factor is how individuals like to send information. When our preferences clash, potential conflict ensues.

Dealing with varying communication preferences complicates the overall structure of the organization. Effective communication should be audience-centered, and while supervisors should not be expected to tailor every message to every individual recipient, creating a culture of general under-standing can help establish a clearer communication climate. To achieve this, though, audits need to be partnered with internal communication strategies.

Developing an Internal Strategy Based on a Communication Audit

The rest of this book will explore the development of internal strategies based on communication audits, but there are several key principles that are appropriate to consider in light of the importance of communication in organizations.

SHARING INFORMATION

When sharing information with employees, you should always provide opportunities for employees to ask additional questions. Employees can do this through direct communication with their manager, human resources, coworkers, and so on. In the big picture, this helps create an environment of cyclical communication and feedback.

MIMIC MEDIA BEST PRACTICES

Internal communication strategies mirror the broad range of mass media available to employees outside of the workplace and integrate the technological evolutions that have infiltrated our daily lives. Furthermore, the strongest internal communication strategies share both good and bad news with honesty and transparency.

DIVERSE WORKFORCE CONSIDERATION

Another important consideration when developing an internal communication strategy is inclusion among a diverse workforce. Roberson (2006) says, "Diversity focuses on organizational demography, whereas inclusion focuses on the removal of obstacles to the full participation and contribution of employees in organizations" (p. 217). In essence, your organizational communication practices should remove obstacles to allow all employees to participate in the organizational conversation.

CHANNELS OF COMMUNICATION

Be strategic in creating the internal communication strategy in order to motivate people to use all channels and mediums that are provided by the organization. However, and this is an important reason why audits are important, organizations must make sure to create and share appropriate content depending on the channel and platform.

WORKPLACE COMMUNICATION PLATFORMS

As an organization develops an internal communication strategy, a consideration of the platform(s) appropriate for each goal should be taken seriously. An internal strategy must incorporate different platforms, recognizing that we must be careful to not overwhelm users with new and different technology but instead use tools that enhance the overall vision of the organization. While it is true that the implementation and assessment of workplace communication platforms have historically been simpler, the communication channel options we have at our disposal are incredible. Platforms generally allow members of an organization to achieve synchronous (real-time) and asynchronous communication. Organizations vary in their needs, but instant messaging, voice and videoconferencing, file transfers, screen sharing, and other real-time options have redefined how we view collaboration. This has enabled workplaces to transfer appropriate operations to remote and virtual contexts and, at the very least, established new workplace norms.

TABLE 3.1   Sample Current Dominant Communication Tools

Tool	Use	Purpose
Slack	Instant team communication platform	Give/receive instant feedback and connect with colleagues
Zapier	Workflow automation	Allows applications to connect seamlessly
Google Drive	File management application	Digital file management tool that allows for synchronous collaboration
Zoom	Videoconferencing application	Allows employees to meet in real time over video
Trello	Project management platform	Use visual cues and aesthetic design to increase group productivity

What Does All This Mean?

Effective internal communication must be part of an organization's holistic
vision. It is not enough to assume that a new tool, platform, or software will
solve communication issues. Instead, we must consider the big picture. Audits
can help organizations:

- **Prioritize communication:** If communication *is* the organization, then
  it cannot be ignored. An audit, at the very least, provides an organization
  with an excuse to assess how, when, and why they are sending messages
  internally. And audits help establish new goals and, if used correctly, a
  unified vision for communication moving forward.

- **Achieve increased effectiveness across organizational initiatives:**
  Audits can be used not only to help establish organizational priorities but
  also to help organizations see where they are succeeding. Effective communication can increase employee engagement and job satisfaction and
  will help employees be more productive.

- **Unify voices:** Whether an organization's messages typically come from supervisors, employers, or even board members, or (most generally) through mass messages via technology platforms, it is still important to unify voices and create mechanisms for empowered understanding. In this vein, an audit can help establish patterns, habits, and communication trends.

- **Satisfy preferences:** While an audit may not be able to identify every communication issue, it can help you establish general baseline expectations of your employees and reach a communication consensus (when you can).

- **Streamline channels:** An audit can identify where a communication platform is, or is not, performing its appropriate duties, thus paving the way for streamlined platforms.

- **Provide constructive dissent:** When employees do not have proper, effective avenues for raising concerns, they are less satisfied and more willing to exit. Further, by raising concerns, organizations can recognize and deal with problems before they are too large in scope and thus damaging. A communication audit can also identify areas where employees do not have channels for expressing upward concern.

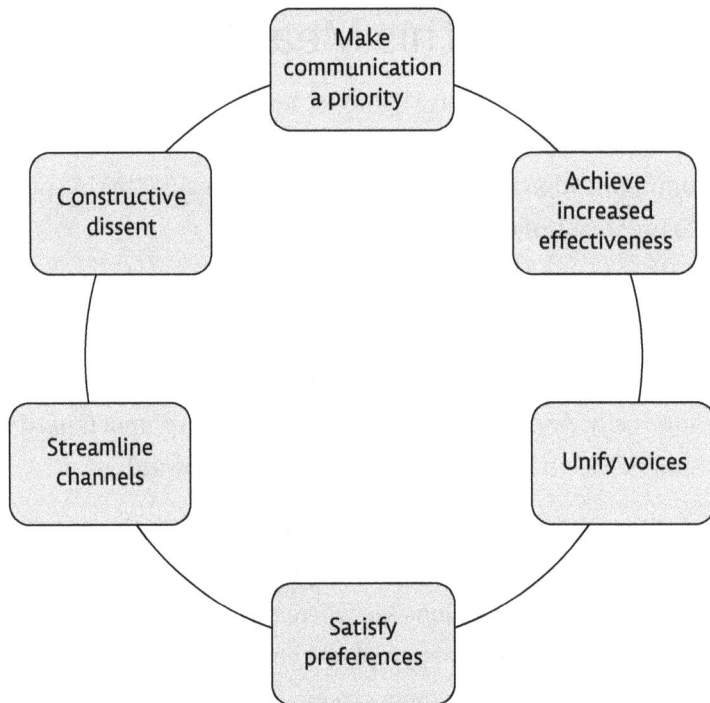

| Figure 3.2 Effective Internal Communication

Communication audits, then, become wonderful tools for assessing communication effectiveness and can help all parties establish a common language and common vision toward increased awareness and effectiveness. Figure 3.2 above is a visual representation of audit benefits. The next chapter will address how to determine what the actual audit process should be and will provide tips for determining which steps need to be involved.

ACTIVITIES AND DISCUSSION QUESTIONS

1. How has communication changed since the COVID-19 pandemic?

_____

_____

_____

_____

_____

_____

2. Why is communication important in the workplace?

_____

_____

_____

_____

_____

_____

3. Have you ever been part of an organization with an internal communication strategy? If so, how did having a strategy help achieve organizational goals?

_____

_____

_____

_____

_____

_____

4. In your opinion, what are some of the most effective communication platforms (e.g., Zoom, Microsoft Teams, Group Me, etc.), and what makes them effective?

_____

_____

_____

_____

_____

_____

WHAT WOULD YOU DO?

Imagine you are an employee at an organization that continues to buy into the newest communication technology. How would you communicate to others in your department or organization at large that these platforms need to be effective and efficient without sacrificing clarity and cohesion?

_____

_____

_____

_____

_____

_____

_____

_____

_____

_____

_____

_____

CHAPTER 4

Determining the Procedure

T his chapter will help you identify a potential audit procedure in the midst of your organizational infrastructure. The content for this chapter will highlight the differing communication needs of organizations with different strategic goals.

The Audit Process

This chapter will explore several qualifying questions. As you determine the direction your audit needs to take, you need to first understand varying organizational needs. The previous chapter explored communication in organizations broadly, and this chapter will take that information and create potential categorizations and steps for conducting an audit and exploring big picture challenges.

The first question you have to ask as you pursue an audit is what you are trying to determine. Specifically, then, you have to ask:

- What do I *need* to measure?

- What do I *want* to measure?

- What situational factors are influencing the organization?

To answer these questions, there should be a general framework that you follow as you work toward audit completion. While an audit can be unique in every context, the process outlined below will help you consider a big picture direction (see Figure 4.1).

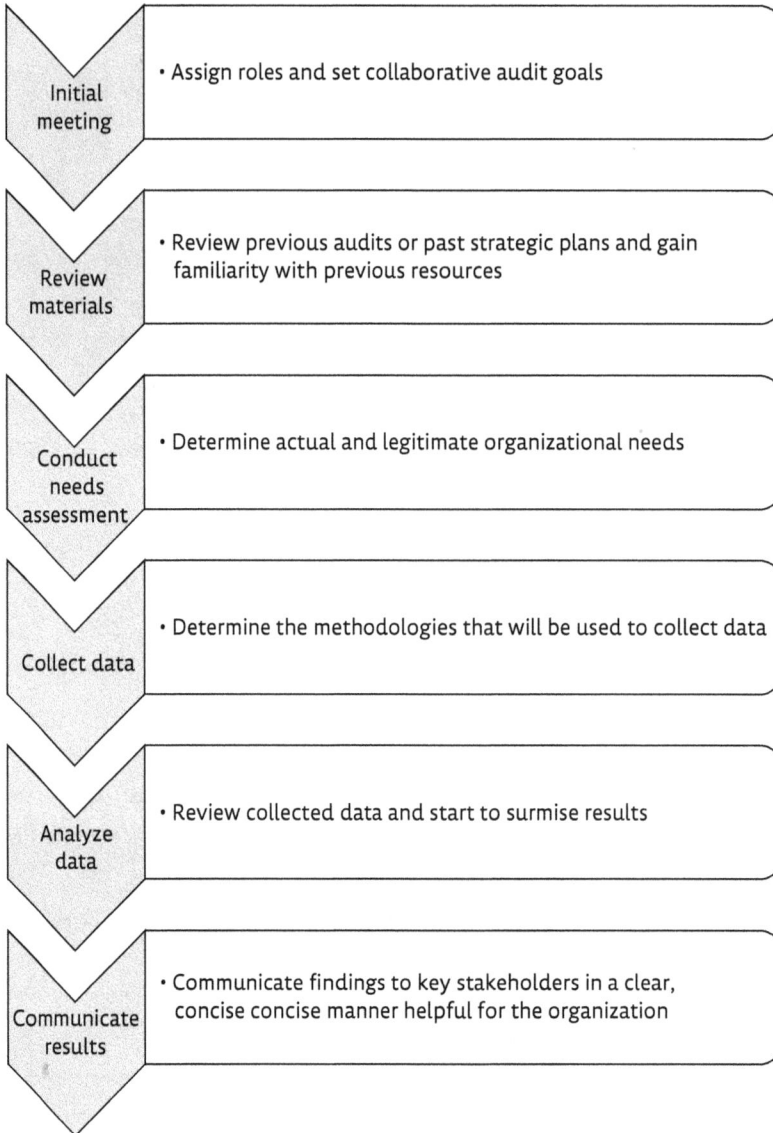

Initial meeting
- Assign roles and set collaborative audit goals

Review materials
- Review previous audits or past strategic plans and gain familiarity with previous resources

Conduct needs assessment
- Determine actual and legitimate organizational needs

Collect data
- Determine the methodologies that will be used to collect data

Analyze data
- Review collected data and start to surmise results

Communicate results
- Communicate findings to key stakeholders in a clear, concise concise manner helpful for the organization

| Figure 4.1 The Audit Process

A General Process

Every audit process will differ depending on the stakeholders involved and the organization's needs. However, there is a general framework and steps to follow as you try to review communication effectiveness and efficiency.

Step 1: Initial consultation and planning meeting.

Objectives:

- **Assign roles.**
  Determine who will be responsible for which audit components.

- **Set collaborative audit goals.**
  Set specific goals that are measurable and attainable. The auditor cannot create the goals alone. There should be a collaborative process to determine what needs the audit will accomplish.

Who is involved:

- **Determine key parties.**
  Generally, the audience will be the consultant (either internal/external) and/or the auditor. In addition, key stakeholders, including the primary client and any key supervisors or project coordinators, will be involved in this step.

Step 2: Review materials.

Objective:

- **Review previous audits or past strategic plans.**
  Familiarize yourself with previous resources.

Step 3: Conduct a needs assessment.

Objective:

- **Determine actual and legitimate organizational needs.**
  These should align with the initial goals, but there may be some variance.

Who is involved:

- **Determine key parties.**
  The consultant/auditor will be the primary voice in this endeavor, but there must be a holistic and system-wide process of organizational discovery. In lay terms, all key parties must be involved as appropriate.

Step 4: Collect data.

Objective:

- **Determine the methodologies you will use to collect data.**
  Surveys, focus groups, in-depth interviews, critical incident analysis, network analyses, and participant observations are all legitimate and potentially necessary data collection methods.

Step 5: Analyze data.

Objective:

- **Review collected data and start to surmise results.**

Step 6: Communicate results.

Objective:

- **Communicate your findings to key stakeholders.**
  This should be done in a clear and concise manner that is helpful and valuable for the organization.

These six steps will encompass most of what happens throughout the audit process. While the audit may veer in different directions depending on need, the movement from initial consultation to the communication of results will be relatively straightforward. Now, with that said, depending on your role and expertise, the organization may have you initiate actual programs or suggestions based on the results you find. But that may not be the case with every completed audit.

Using Available Data

As you enter into the audit process, use the resources currently at your disposal to articulate in your own mind what potential next steps may be. Effective analysts will use any available data to help clarify potential needs, even before the initial consultation. Thankfully, even before you sit down with a potential client or internally with your supervisors to discuss the direction of an audit, some information is probably already available to you. As you consider the process, you need to determine what sources of data are presently accessible. For instance:

- Has the organization developed an employee survey addressing communication? If so, when was that survey last distributed? If the survey is recent, can you have access to past results? Even if a survey is not recent, valuable information may be available.

- Are you able to access current policies and procedures? An organization may have a communication plan in place. If there is a current plan, you need access to any identifiable materials that were used to build the plan or that have been used to measure its effectiveness.

- Do you have access to any previous audits that the organization has developed in the past, and even more importantly, do you have access to those results? You may be able to find a few incredible nuggets of information that can help you achieve your current audit goals more effectively and efficiently.

There may be data sources that exist outside of the previous survey realm and that have been developed separately from a previous audit context (e.g., exit interview data). As you consider immediate next steps, your primary role is that of observer and researcher. You want to understand as much background information as you can about any potential audit client. As such, you want to make sure you are researching any stories about the organization (e.g., news media stories) that have been reported and having conversations with those who are familiar with the organization. As you navigate through this initial observational phase, you will enter the goal setting step with greater clarity. This background information will help you converse more intelligently with stakeholders and will be invaluable as you create your plan for the initial needs assessment.

Setting Goals

Chapter 5 will discuss in more depth the role of the auditor in the initial planning meeting. However, it is worth noting here that setting collaborative goals is a necessary part of the preliminary process. The auditor should not be the only one setting organizational goals. Instead, goal setting should be a collaborative process where key stakeholders identify outcomes and work with the auditors to streamline those ideas. There are different contexts where this may not be the case. For instance, if an organization has an internal communication staff and works hard to execute a communication plan, there may be embedded goals that do not need senior-level identification. In this case, the auditor would probably be an internal employee who has familiarity with the strategic plan. However, most organizations may not have resources to conduct an internal audit led by their own people on a consistent basis.

Strategic organizational communication goals may:

- Improve trust within the organization between employees and managers.

- Improve productivity by streamlining communication and removing communication efforts that are redundant, unclear, or time consuming.

- Create repositories and mechanisms for employees to find information in a timely and effective manner.

- Increase employee engagement.

- Increase employee satisfaction (i.e., morale).

- Clarify the organization's mission and vision and communicate these ideals to employees to increase employees' sense of connectedness to the organization.

- Decrease misunderstanding across the organization.

- Increase opportunities for employees to offer feedback to the organization.

This list is not exhaustive, but identifying some strategic goals will help the auditor and key stakeholders find common ground and plan for the audit.

Remember, at this phase it is important to secure senior-level leadership endorsement or buy-in. Procuring this buy-in can happen by enlisting the right stakeholders and key gatekeepers in the goal-setting process.

QUESTION

In what other ways can strategic organizational communication goals be useful?

_____

_____

_____

_____

_____

_____

One of the things that makes conducting an audit so difficult is the disconnect between key leadership/management and employees. As you navigate the audit process, you must be a funnel. Senior leadership will communicate their audit goals to you. They may see big picture issues or, in some cases, have presuppositions that the audit can address. It is helpful to take these suggestions into account while also realizing that the audit will bring to light challenges and concerns. The initial collaborative goals should be developed in such a way that the audit's purpose is clearly defined without assuming what findings the audit will present. As the auditor, then, you must be an active listener and observer. Listen intently to senior leadership as they share their concerns while also recognizing that their perspective may be tainted.

The perspective, also, of the broader employee base may be inaccurate as well. There are bigger picture concerns that many in the organization may not understand, and this lack of knowledge may cloud their judgment.

Because of the potential disconnect, strategic communication goals become extremely important. The potential goals listed here are helpful for establishing a baseline foundation. As you think about the big picture, though, an organization's strategic communication goals may fall under one of three general categories: strategy, implementation, and integration.

Strategy

As you think about strategic communication at your organization, you must first think about where you want to go. There is an element here of forward thinking. You must think about how the overall vision of the organization and the communication vision align and then consider how the goals help to achieve this vision. Your goals, then, extrapolate out to incorporate messages and delivery mechanisms, actual messengers, as well as communication channels. This higher level thinking gives the auditor and the stakeholders something to aspire to.

Implementation

The implementation category helps us consider how we get there. Specifically, this is where messages are actually created and where you train or retrain employees to respond to appropriate messages and materials. Evaluation is also a crucial part of this phase, as you will want to monitor communication activities and outcomes to determine how effectively these have connected to the strategic goals.

Integration

The integration step is foundational but sometimes overlooked. Think of integration as the network. There has to be a mechanism for integrating communication throughout all levels of the organization. The integration phase is the support framework that helps make sure all communication platforms are working effectively and that sufficient resources have been secured.

As you determine the audit process, think about where you want to go. Your strategic goals will probably fall under one of these categories:

- Is there a holistic issue with strategy?

- Is the big picture vision for communication not aligned with the organization's goals?

- Is there an issue with implementation?

- Is the organization not developing effective messaging, or have employees received too little training?

The issue could also be related to integration. The organization, in this case, does not have the appropriate tools to get the job done. At this phase, key leadership or stakeholders may not show adequate understanding or support of broader communication initiatives and refuse to see communication as integral to organizational success.

Determining where the disconnect is in the broader structure—either strategy, implementation, or integration—will help you determine what you need to measure.

At the beginning of this chapter, I made note of the fact that understanding what you want to determine, or know, is crucial for an auditor. For one, you need to see some semblance of an end goal. Your clients, both internal and external, want to know that there is light at the end of the tunnel and that you, as facilitator of the audit, will work to achieve these goals. With that being said, there are different appropriations you have to consider as you identify how you want the audit to commence. It is important to have a general framework in your mind about the audit process and to know how to structure the strategic goals conversation. You also need to distinguish between what is absolutely necessary to measure/assess and what is more of a luxury.

What Do I Need to Measure?

As you consider what you need to measure, you have to step back and consider senior-level priorities. As mentioned, the client will have specific ideas about what the issues may be and how to solve these concerns. Your job, as the auditor, is to develop an assessment that can incorporate the feedback of senior-level administrators without relying solely on their feedback and desires. This is hard to do, but a proper needs assessment can help you differentiate between senior-level concerns from challenges that exist throughout the organization.

As you consider what you need to measure, it is important to answer general questions on behalf of the organization:

- **Who is the targeted audience?** Different segments of target audiences will have varying needs. An audit will help segment different stakeholder/audience needs.

- **What are the communication objectives or goals?** These goals will often tie directly back to individual audience members or stakeholder groups.

- **How are "we" (the organization) currently communicating?** What tools, platforms, processes, and procedures are used to communicate at the moment?

These questions are important to answer as you plan your audit process. It is not enough to just select randomized assessments that may provide insight. Instead, there must be a mapping process where the auditor and the stakeholders work together to achieve goals and measure objectives.

For an audit to effectively measure communication, you must first identify what you actually want to learn. Are you looking to target employee perceptions about the organization at large, find information about communication preferences and individual styles, or even measure the effectiveness of individual tools or platforms? Without a proper understanding of where you are going, you cannot determine how to get there.

Once you have identified exactly what you want to learn, you need to solicit buy-in from the appropriate stakeholders. More on this phenomenon will be discussed in the next chapter. Generally, though, you want to make sure that you have secured support from those who control the budget and those who are change agents (i.e., the ones who can actually influence the organization).

A clear plan of exactly what you need to assess with a rationale for different ideas can help you garner support.

What Do I Want to Measure?

As you assess the communication situation of an organization, you will have opportunities to explore hunches. Chapter 2 emphasized the role of the consultant because anyone who performs an audit or assessment function in an organization is, in some form or fashion, a consultant and in many cases is probably a subject matter expert. Obviously, this may not be the case in every audit circumstance. However, if you are a subject matter expert and believe you have some insight into additional areas that are worth exploring, it may be helpful to bring those into the audit. But you must distinguish needs from wants.

As you conduct an audit, you want to make sure that you have appropriated the time and resources needed to complete the job. An audit can be time consuming, stressful, and expensive. Therefore, approaching the necessary components of an audit should be the top priority. However, as you review previous data, observe general organizational behavior, and have conversations with stakeholders, you may have an educated guess as to what additional periphery issues may be causing communication confusion in the organization. When I interact with clients, I call these my "audit wants." In some ways, these may be budgetary add-ons for an organization, but if there are more holistic concerns, then your role, as the auditor, is to partly communicate any additional steps you can take to identify other issues. Much of this depends on the client and the organization. In some cases, an organization will have a very clear determination already established related to what they want the audit to accomplish, and because of resources or some other reason, they may not want to veer from those determinations. Yet I always like to build in a buffer where I can articulate, based on my experience, some issues that may be worth assessing that may not fit within the concrete scope of those nonnegotiable elements we absolutely have to address.

Situational Context

While needs and wants are certainly important, as the one conducting the audit, you must also be aware of any situational issues that impact the organization.

While there may be additional situational issues that arise, there are four primary considerations you should address as you discern environmental factors influencing your audit plans. I have categorized these situational factors as culture, competition, context, and values.

CULTURE

An organization's culture includes several factors. Primarily, the culture of an organization includes its norms, or how the organization functions. Culture is deeply embedded and, for our purposes, can be hard to overcome. In most organizations, the cultural distinctions are top-down and hierarchical. Key stakeholders and leaders tend to dictate the culture. For audit purposes, it is hard to overcome distinct cultural elements that have been developed over time, especially negative elements like turf battles or power struggles. Yet audits can help provide a rationale for change. Here are a few questions to consider when overcoming culture as a situational factor.

Questions to Consider

1. Are there distinct communication preferences across the organization?

2. What organizational norms are present that dictate communication?

3. What facets about how this organization communicates are cultural (e.g., answering emails throughout the evening, avoiding conflict, etc.)?

COMPETITION

For our purposes, culture is internal. It is defined and developed throughout the organization. There are, however, outside forces working to influence communication. One primary external element is competition. While some have said that imitation is the sincerest form of flattery, it may not be the most effective means for determining how an organization operates. However, some organizations will be tempted to structure their communication efforts solely based on what their competition is doing, figuring that "if it works for them, it will work for us." This is hard to overcome because you have to convince members of the organization that their workplace is unique, filled with different people, and that just because a competitor enacts a certain practice does not mean that it will work for them.

Questions to Consider

1. What communication efforts have been modeled after competing entities?

2. Do communication efforts have a strategic plan or evaluative measures?

3. What may be different about competing organizations that will not apply in this specific case?

CONTEXT

Context can be both internal and external. At the time of this writing, the world is reeling from a global pandemic that changed almost every aspect of our lives. Some workplaces, for instance, went from face-to-face operations to entirely virtual environments. The pandemic is a contextual factor. It is environmental, outside of the realm of control for organizations, yet has a significant impact on communication style. Context can be policy based, environmental, or historical (i.e., happening at a specific point in time). Audits should account for contextual factors.

Questions to Consider

1. What forces are exerting their influence on the organization and have modified communication efforts?

2. What contextual factors are unique to the current audit process?

VALUES

The organization, sometimes without meaning to, displays cultural values to their clients, internal stakeholders, and constituents. These core values should be ethical and exemplify a mission/vision-driven mantra. Yet, as is often the case, the organization's displayed values may not align with their stated values.

A communication audit can help organizations determine their core values and help communicate these core values to the organization at large.

Questions to Consider

1. How may an audit help reveal an organization's core values?

2. In what ways do the values of an organization reveal what the organization cares about?

The important thing to remember is that the audit process can be fluid and flexible. Every organization has different stakeholders and unique strategic goals. As such, the audit becomes less about a concrete and rigid framework and more about adapting certain best practices to fit organizational needs. The role of the auditor, then, is to determine the audit procedure based on all of the competing factors discussed here and then to garner support and buy-in from stakeholders across the organization.

ACTIVITIES AND DISCUSSION QUESTIONS

1. Which communication goals may be most important to your organization at this point in time?

_____

_____

_____

_____

_____

_____

2. Is any data currently available that your organization has that can shed light on any big picture communication issues?

_____

_____

_____

_____

_____

_____

3. What situational factors exist that complicate communication in your organization?

_____

_____

_____

_____

_____

_____

WHAT WOULD YOU DO?

Imagine your organization has been dealing with personnel-driven relationship conflict (this can be either task oriented or personality based). The organization has come to you to help gather data related to job satisfaction, identity, and interpersonal dynamics. Briefly, answer the three key questions from this chapter as you think about what you would do:

1. What do I need to measure?

2. What do I want to measure?

3. What situational factors are influencing the organization?

CHAPTER 5

Involving Stakeholders

This chapter will help you think about how to involve stakeholders in the audit process, specifically managers, executives, employees, clients, and customers. The content for this chapter will serve as a brief audience analysis of sorts to help you determine who to speak with throughout the audit process, which stakeholders to meet with to secure buy-in, and how to establish clear communication to make sure the stakeholders feel appropriately involved.

Without buy-in from key stakeholders, an audit may be fruitless. Throughout the audit process, as you determine what you need to measure, you may be tasked with interviewing senior managers, communication staff, or other key members of the organization. Interviews, focus groups, and surveys can be time-consuming (and expensive) endeavors. But even before you start collecting data from different stakeholder groups, you need to establish a connection with those who are active participants in the process and, even more so, those who need to see value in the audit process.

Considering the time and financial costs of an audit, an organization, especially a larger organization, should be willing to potentially designate tens of thousands of dollars, not to mention the sheer amount of company time, to an audit completion. However, as the organization strives for greater efficiency, the payoff will be worth it. To not waste the organization's time, you need to begin the process of determining which stakeholders need to be involved in the process.

Determining Stakeholders

Typically, an audit process will begin in a similar manner to a consultation. The auditor will either approach or be approached by the potential client. In some ways, this establishes a clear direct report. The main contact will probably become your primary gatekeeper. It is important, though, to recognize that there are others involved in this process.

An astute auditor will recognize that stakeholders have different roles. Generally, during an audit, you will interact with key individuals who have different organizational responsibilities. At the most basic level, you will interact with employees (internally) and the general public (externally). The next level of stakeholders are those managers, supervisors, or other key leaders who may not be considered primary but still have valuable voices to contribute to the process. The most immediate or primary stakeholders are those who have the most vested, usually financial, interest in the audit. Primary stakeholders include those who are paying for the audit or to whom the auditor reports results. A board, CFO, CEO, or other chief officers may be considered primary stakeholders.

Stakeholders (i.e., those individuals or groups that have an interest in activities or decisions made by an organization) at these levels will exert different layers of influence across the organization. External consultants are usually considered subject matter experts. However, the organization will also have subject matter experts who can contribute necessary information. Subject matter experts can cross departments or organizational hierarchy. Part of what the auditor must accomplish is to tap into subject matter expertise that exists throughout the organization. Assessment of the organization should begin with an assessment of key voices that can contribute to the audit.

Questions to Consider

1. In your immediate interactions with the client, what is the expectation of the scope of the audit? The scope will determine how widespread your stakeholder interaction needs to be.

2. Are there gatekeepers across the organization that wield great influence?

3. In your initial meetings, are there individuals who the client or board considers to be key voices?

As you consider these questions, remember that the scope and strategic audit goals will determine who to involve and at what capacity. You may need to focus on individuals or entire departments. The audit process will gradually include additional stakeholders as the auditor finds out more information about potential communication challenges. It is important not to be selective about key voices, recognizing that the potential for repetitive concerns is a real issue.

The focus of this text is primarily on internal stakeholders because the topic surrounds conducting internal communication audits. There may be times, though, where you need to interact with external stakeholders. If this is the case, many of the same elements apply; however, the focus becomes less about the internal workings of the communication dynamic and more about how the message is communicated and received outside of the organization.

One final note about determining stakeholders: An internal auditor may not have the luxury of remaining objective, although that should be the goal. An external auditor, however, must remain an objective assessor. Avoid becoming too connected to individuals or individual opinions. Instead, consider the spectrum of voices and give credence to credible perspectives. Your ability to discern how credible stakeholders' voices will be helped along by setting up meetings with stakeholders early and often.

ACTIVITY

A stakeholder table is included below. Use the tool to determine who needs to be involved in the needs assessment and data collection portion of the audit. A generic sample has been included in the first row, and a more specific sample has been included in the second row.

Individual or department	Audit value	Level of involvement	Communication	Receptiveness/resistance/concerns
Name	What value will this individual or department add to the audit process?	Indicate how involved this individual or department needs to be. Rank their potential involvement from 1 (minimal involvement) to 5 (significant involvement).	Have you communicated with this department, and in what capacity?	Indicate how receptive this individual or department may be from 1 (resistant) to 5 (very receptive). Include any potential concerns as well.
Human resources	Can provide insight into personnel and employee engagement	5	Communication occurred on May 5th; Focus groups and in-depth interviews	4

(continued)

DISCOVERY SESSION

The initial meeting with a client, whether internal or external, may take different forms. However, the first interaction will usually involve some form of discovery. A discovery session should accomplish exactly what the name implies: a chance to understand the context and hear about initial expectations. In theory, you are all discovering whether or not this partnership will be a good fit. Remember, the more you involve stakeholders early in the audit process, the more buy-in you can get when you have to make recommendations or changes later on.

Especially in the communication audit world, a discovery session can be a great place to determine whether or not an audit is needed or if there are other ways to solve potentially complex problems. As a communication consultant and trainer, I have found that most clients will bring me in because they have a communication problem, not because they want me to conduct an audit. Yet the audit is how we determine what the problem really is and how to solve it. Therefore, in many ways, the client is asking for an audit to be completed without even knowing it. For this reason, I like to have a mini pitch ready that summarizes what an audit can do and provide an overview of how it can be helpful.

If you want to craft a more in-depth audit description, I encourage you to revisit Chapter 1. However, I am including my audit overview below to help offer some context.

ACTIVITY

Have you ever heard of something called a "communication audit"? Basically, it allows us to pinpoint communication issues you are experiencing. Right now it sounds like relational conflict is a significant problem, and it may be, but my guess is there are other issues happening below the surface that you may not even be aware of. By conducting an audit, I can assess needs and collect data that will give us the true source(s) of communication breakdown that may be impacting morale or even productivity.

Use the space below to craft your own audit elevator pitch:

_____

_____

_____

_____

_____

_____

Discovery sessions can be valuable for reasons other than positioning the audit as a problem-identifying assessment. You will probably find through initial conversations that occur via email, phone, or even through a project enquiry form that end goals may be hard to identify. If you can tell your client is a little unclear about what they need or want from you, a discovery session can help everyone get on the same page and start the conversation to align goals and objectives. To summarize, a discovery session, or initial consultation, can be helpful for many reasons:

- As mentioned in the previous chapter, meetings can help the auditor and key leaders identify shared goals or outcomes.

- Management may have ideas about individuals who should be involved in focus groups or interviews as well as departments or groups of employees who should be surveyed.

- Meeting attendees may be able to help identify potential barriers to a successful audit completion.

- Stakeholders can help provide access to information including but not limited to previous communication or strategic plans.

- An initial consultation can help everyone clarify expectations including but not limited to overall budget and time to completion.

I like for the discovery phase to be conversational. I wait until the needs assessment, covered in Chapter 6, to uncover existing documents, determine who to interview, and identify other data collection that may be needed. There are different questions you need to ask during the discovery session.

Questions to Consider

1. Who has commissioned the audit? Has it been requested from the board, a key leader, or another stakeholder?

2. If there has been contact that occurred prior to the discovery session, how did the discovery session remain consistent with the initial contact? In what ways has the conversation during the discovery session veered from previous interactions?

MEETING WITH STAKEHOLDERS

Auditors can secure buy-in, in part, by directly asking stakeholders for feedback or ideas. An initial consultation or planning meeting can help define who needs to be involved in the audit process and in what capacity. There is a delicate balance here because senior-level management will have their own ideas about what is "wrong" with the organization. You must take their recommendations, secure their buy-in, and still feel confident in your own expertise. What key leaders think is wrong may not be what is actually hindering communication within the organization.

This puts the consultant or one crafting the audit in a precarious position. You are living in two worlds: subject matter expert and paid employee. You are meant to be objective, yet you also have been brought into the fold by specific members of the organization, meaning you "answer" to someone. Living in this gray area requires wise and discerning meeting construction. You must not rely on improvisation during a meeting and instead should think strategically about how you lead and observe meetings during the audit process.

LEADING A MEETING

Just like any corporate setting, a meeting where you, the consultant or auditor, meet with clients should be well prepared and thought out. As such, you should have an agenda and a clear purpose. The most frustrating meetings are those where a purpose has not been stated beforehand, and as the leader of the meeting, it is your responsibility to keep the meeting on track and ready to meet objectives. Setting an agenda helps you stay focused and shows the client that the meeting is moving somewhere. A meeting agenda is also a level of accountability for you, as it allows you to know that you have not veered off course. There are several types of meetings you may have to initiate or lead as the auditor:

- **Progress/status update:** Let the client know where the project is at its current phase.

- **Information sharing:** Cues the client in on key recent developments.

- **Decision making:** Client and consultant work together to make an actual decision about next steps.

- **Problem solving:** Client and consultant work together to solve a distinct problem.

- **Innovation:** Client and consultant work together to come up with a new or innovative approach to a concept related to the audit.

When leading a meeting, it is important to have an end goal. Understanding what you plan to get out of the meeting will inform which type of meeting needs to occur. While it may be impossible at times, especially if you have limited face time with the client, try not to combine meeting purposes. Instead, make the meeting shorter and more focused.

Thankfully, a focused meeting tends to have an agenda. An effective agenda will not be created in a vacuum; usually, you should solicit input about what needs to be covered. The agenda items should focus on the stakeholders in attendance, meaning you should not present problems or questions that those in attendance cannot answer. Finally, make sure you estimate, accurately, how much time you need to complete each agenda item. Do not shortchange discussion or the decision-making process. Instead, think realistically about how much time you should devote to each item you plan to address.

45-Minute Meeting Sample Agenda

10:00–10:05 Welcome and important announcements/updates

10:05–10:20 Project updates

10:20–10:30 Project needs (how the organization or your leaders can help you achieve your goals)

10:30–10:45 Action steps/accountability for next meeting

Quick Tips: Leading a Meeting

Before the meeting:

1. Prepare (what needs to happen, what decisions need to be made, what actions need to occur).

2. Conduct effectively by keeping everyone on task and engaged.

During the meeting:

3. Establish ground rules.

4. Highlight transitions, summarize, and then follow-up afterward.

After the meeting:

5. Give exceptionally clear action steps.

Remember, determine if a meeting is necessary before calling people together, then have a clear agenda and maintain focus throughout the agenda.

OBSERVING A MEETING

When completing a communication audit, you should familiarize yourself with communication across the organization in every format. The tendency for some will be to focus on text-based documents and for good reason. Those tend to illuminate processes and procedures. However, you also need to observe both informal interpersonal interactions (relational interactions between a small number of coworkers or employees/employers) as well as more formal interactions, like meetings.

Meetings represent the communication ebb and flow of organizations. These interactions can occur in face-to-face or virtual settings with anywhere from two members to hundreds, if not thousands, in attendance. Meetings tend to be the lifeblood of how members within organizations interact, and while electronic forms of instant communication have drastically changed how we communicate in the workplace, meetings still cause challenges.

A consultant, then, may have to observe meetings at varying levels to understand if the communication happening in these formal settings is effective and purposeful. When observing a meeting, you are just that: an observer. You need to take clear notes, remain silent, and try to wisely understand what challenges exist within the meeting space.

Observing is obviously different from leading. When you observe a meeting, you should pay special attention to:

- Interactions between coworkers and interactions between employees/employers:

  - Are the interactions civil?

  - Are the interactions forced or awkward?

  - Are attendees interactive?

  - Are attendees respectful?

- Process and procedure:

  - Does the meeting have a clear procedure?

  - Is there a clear leader?

  - Are there clear steps for achieving action items?

  - Does the group have rules for interaction or feedback?

- Outcomes:

  - Does the meeting end with clear next steps?

  - Do attendees seem confused or frustrated?

You will want to announce before the meeting that you will be observing. This may cause attendees to be on their best behavior, but you will gain more credibility.

We will discuss final reports later on, but your meeting observations should be included in your final report. Think strategically about what you observed that could have an impact on communication or even culture.

STAKEHOLDER ENGAGEMENT

The discovery session and individual meetings with stakeholders can be extremely helpful throughout the audit process. But we need to take a more holistic and more active approach when involving stakeholders in the communication audit process and a consultant can help identify those big picture challenges and even offer solutions. Remind yourself that stakeholders can be extremely helpful. If you are conducting an audit as an external consultant, internal stakeholders can help you understand key issues more clearly, and as the discovery session shows, they can help refine goals. Stakeholders can also help identify big picture next steps, like training and development. How you involve stakeholders will influence your interactions with them.

In the section on meetings earlier in this chapter, several different types of meetings were presented: progress/status update, information sharing, decision making, problem solving, and innovation. In some ways, these categories represent how you should involve stakeholders and at what level you need to continually do so. I have streamlined these ideas to more accurately reflect how you should involve stakeholders throughout the process:

Stakeholder	Engagement type	Level of involve-ment	Involvement frequency	Receptiveness/resistance/concerns
Who is involved?	*Inform, feedback, make decisions, solve problems, innovate and initiate*	*1 (minimal) to 5 (significant)*	*Daily, weekly, monthly meetings, etc.*	*1 (resistant) to 5 (very receptive)*
Human resources	Solve problems	4	Weekly meetings with the human resources director	5

Source: https://pressbooks.bccampus.ca/technicalwriting/chapter/stakeholderengagement/

Not all stakeholders may want to be engaged. Part of the process, as you seek to complete the audit, is to determine how involved stakeholders want to be and how involved you need them to be. Organizations are full of power dynamics, and you will need the gatekeepers to help you collect data and to achieve actual change within the organization. However, how stakeholders are engaged throughout the process depends on the strategic goals of the audit.

In the table above, I have given you different types or levels of engagement. Below I provide more detailed descriptions of these engagement types. The key here is to both understand who needs to be involved and at what capacity.

- **Inform:** Informing stakeholders involves information transfer. You are providing them with objective information they ask for, need, or that you may find valuable for them. Your information should be purposeful and should help them understand the audit end goals and what problems you are addressing. Information can be distributed as frequently as the stakeholder desires, but you may find consistent touch points and updates helpful. Your final report will contain the most information.

- **Feedback:** The feedback engagement level is focused on receiving information from the stakeholder, usually about information that has been presented. Feedback can be minimal or in depth. Engagement here can be either regular and consistent or occur less frequently.

Inform and feedback assume a relatively passive participation by the stakeholder. These levels tend to focus more on immediate transfer and guidance. But the final three levels of engagement are much more in depth and collaborative.

- **Make decisions:** This level of engagement involves the stakeholder in decision making either about the audit or next steps. Stakeholders who help make decisions will share their concerns consistently and will work directly with you to continue reaching a solution.

- **Solve problems:** During the process, several challenges may arise either with how the audit is developed or immediate issues related to findings. Stakeholders who help solve problems will provide insight into audit goals and may also work with you to solve problems that may arise.

- **Innovate and initiate:** Finally, stakeholders may be involved at an extremely high level to innovate and think of out-of-the-box ideas and then would be responsible for initiating what they deem as important endeavors. This, again, does not negate the consultant role and instead provides a more collaborative relationship.

No matter the type of engagement, I believe the goal is not to achieve consensus; instead ,the goal is to use stakeholder expertise to craft and conduct an effective audit and, ultimately, implement new practices that will help create streamlined communication processes for the organization. Think strategically about how you can involve stakeholders from the beginning so they can be a valuable part of the process.

ACTIVITIES AND DISCUSSION QUESTIONS

1. Use the space below to create your own meeting agenda:

Time	Agenda item and action steps/accountability

2. List any stakeholders in your organization who should be involved in any audit process, and discuss any value they bring to the organization.

_____

_____

_____

_____

_____

_____

3. Is there anything you would do differently when conducting or observing a virtual meeting versus a physical/face-to-face meeting?

_____

_____

_____

_____

_____

_____

WHAT WOULD YOU DO?

Imagine you are meeting with the next round of stakeholders after the initial discovery session. As a reminder, the initial summary session will probably include those who find the audit valuable or recognize a need (i.e., many stakeholders may not be so aligned). In this scenario, you have been approached about assessing communication efficiency that moves downward (meaning communication from supervisors to supervisees). Plan a meeting with these potentially negative stakeholders. How can you communicate the challenge without being offensive? How can you position the audit as valuable?

_____

_____

_____

_____

_____

_____

_____

_____

_____

_____

_____

PART II

The Communication Audit Process

CHAPTER 6

The Process, Step 1: Needs Assessment

This chapter will reinforce the concept of the needs assessment. To align with strategic organizational goals, a needs assessment is a viable first step to determine how (and, honestly, what) to measure in regard to communication effectiveness.

Communication Audit Process

For our purposes in this book, I am highlighting four distinct steps in the audit process.

Step 1: Needs assessment
Step 2: Data collection and methodology
Step 3: Analyzing data and clarifying results
Step 4: Communicating the results

Generally, the purpose of the needs assessment is to define the problem. Step 2, data collection, is where you collect evidence to show that the problem exists and to what capacity. In Step 3, the data you collected in Step 2 is analyzed and the purpose identified. Finally, Step 4 includes communicating the results to the stakeholders. What follows after the results are communicated, the actual corresponding initiatives, are not considered part of the audit process and instead exist separately as an action step for the organization (this is discussed in more detail later in this book).

This chapter focuses exclusively on the needs assessment process.

What Is a Needs Assessment?

Kaufman and Guerra-Lopez (2013) wisely distinguish between two different audit types: a training audit and a performance audit. A training audit has a predisposed recognition that training provides the necessary solution. Training can be extremely helpful. Communication audits, for instance, may reveal training needs related to employee engagement, supervisor–subordinate rapport, relationship building, conflict management, or any number of other issues. Training can help solve deep-rooted issues in organizations, and a training needs assessment helps the consultant know what issues need to be solved and how training can help. On the other hand, a performance audit is a bit more tactical.

A needs assessment can provide data related to gaps in results. If a gap exists, a needs assessment should tell us where the issue resides, and a needs analysis will provide information regarding the causes of certain issues. If you think back to our earlier discussion about strategic goals, a needs assessment can help you determine what *is* compared to what *should be* (Altschuld & Watkins, 2014) and immediately provides insight into how to spend the remaining audit time. The initial assessment is a crucial step because it helps identify areas or challenges that need to be resolved. And on a more practical note, it saves the organization money and the consultant time.

Altschuld and Watkins (2014) offer certain questions a needs assessment should address:

- What results should be accomplished at the societal, organizational, and individual levels?

- How do current results relate to desired results?

- How should we think about diverse needs in terms of importance?

- Which alternative solution strategies (or sets of solutions) can best reduce gaps in results?

- What criteria can be used to evaluate the alternatives?

A needs assessment will help you determine where to focus your audit. The questions above help provide a clear focus, which is essential. Organizations are looking for results, and your role, as either an internal or external consultant or general communication manager, is to help the organization achieve their desired results. The needs assessment will reveal a gap where the desired result is not being met. Your role, then, is to highlight why the gap exists and potentially offer solutions for what to do to solve the problem. Some will call this a "needs analysis." We call it a "communication audit."

One great resource for needs assessment development is Witkin's (1984) book *Assessing Needs in Educational and Social Programs*. In it, Witkin identifies three different phases of a needs assessment: pre-assessment, assessment, and post-assessment (see Figure 6.1).

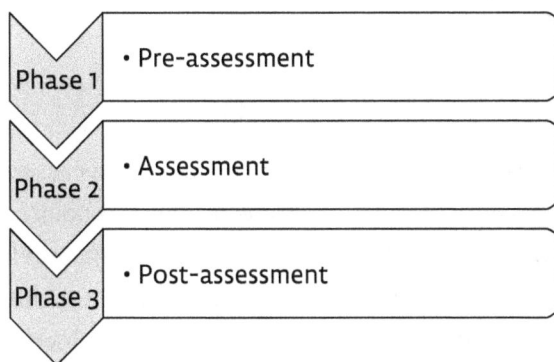

| Figure 6.1 The Three Phases of a Needs Assessment

PHASE 1: PRE-ASSESSMENT

Phase 1 relies primarily on preexisting data (e.g., previous assessment results, exit interview data, external news media stories, etc.). This is similar to what we would find in an initial consultation or even a document review. The pre-assessment step is concerned with context and determining, albeit broadly, if a need actually does exist. At this point, though, you will not be defining the need, just recognizing, based on current data, that there is some need. Pre-assessment extant data may include previous surveys, exit interview data, media reports, and so forth.

PHASE 2: ASSESSMENT

The actual assessment, Phase 2, occurs after the pre-assessment is completed. Phase 2 is a more in-depth search. Theoretically, you would build on what you found in Phase 1 and potentially conduct interviews or have in-depth conversations with additional stakeholders. Witkins (1984) rightly recognizes that this phase may address a causal analysis of needs and even a prioritization of needs. The assessment phase is where you would start gathering some foundational information.

PHASE 3: POST-ASSESSMENT

Phase 3 of the needs assessment process, the post-assessment, is used to determine next steps. At this point in a communication audit, you would have the primary need(s) identified and then determine different methods to collect additional data. During Phase 3 you will also evaluate the actual needs assessment itself.

Needs Assessment Process

There is some debate about the actual process of a needs assessment. To be honest, some of the issues are semantic. Some reading this book could consider the communication audit itself to be a needs assessment, and in some ways this is correct. However, I believe the needs assessment is the preliminary discovery analysis that then propels you toward data collection to uncover and unearth systemic organizational communication-related issues. The needs assessment, then, becomes the way that you determine what and how to study the organization.

The needs assessment process can consist of many steps. I want to highlight three relatively distinct concepts that occur throughout the assessment process.

INFORMATION GATHERING

The information-gathering step consists very literally of gathering as much preliminary information as possible. Again, and not to belabor the point, this could be achieved through meetings with initial stakeholders, document review, observation, or other means. The point here is that you are trying not to determine a need without first doing due diligence to understand if the need actually exists. If you plan your audit under a false assumption, it will fall flat and not be effective, and your clients will not be satisfied with data collection that does not address the underlying problem. This step may also be called an "external and organizational scan."

ANALYSIS

Once you have gathered as much information as you can, you need to analyze these potential needs. Determine where you see patterns, themes, and holistic trends. At this step you need to recognize different inconsistencies. For example, are you hearing different wants from different stakeholders, or have you heard various issues communicated in conflicting ways? Generally, a needs analysis will define deficiencies and articulate some felt value. There will potentially be numerous issues at an organization, especially related to communication. Your role is to prioritize. To understand which needs have the most value, return back to the strategic goals the stakeholder(s) identified.

The following questions will help you analyze potential needs.

Questions to Consider

1. What level of outcome or performance is expected?
2. Is there a gap in performance?
3. What are the potential causes of these gaps?
4. What additional information is needed to address the issue?

Your role as the assessor, after reviewing preliminary information, is to assess potential needs and to try to evaluate them based on order of importance. Additionally, you need to determine what you can actually achieve within the scope and confines of the audit. Do not try to solve every issue at once.

DETERMINATION

Once you have collected preliminary information and analyzed these apparent needs, you should then determine which needs your audit can and should address. This is, yet again, a conversation that happens with the client and stakeholders. As you determine which needs to address or try to address in your audit, it is important to remember that stakeholders will have different values and that you also may see matters of more importance compared to those who are working with you on the project or those who have solicited your expertise. When this is the case, I tend to add additional measures or items in surveys or ask additional questions in interviews of focus groups that resonate with those other needs. This does not have to be a substantial part of your audit, but if you have a hunch and want to see if your initial considerations are accurate, do not be afraid to test these assumptions throughout the audit process. I give the same advice to stakeholders. If there is something they really believe is an issue and it is not revealed as a major or urgent need throughout the needs assessment, you may be able to measure this issue without adding substantial time or energy to the audit process.

Types of Needs Assessments

While there are other needs assessment types that have evolved, two remain most important: the training needs assessment and performance needs assessment. I would like to add a third crucial focus: the organizational needs assessment.

TRAINING NEEDS ASSESSMENT

A training needs assessment has, as its end goal, professional development for employees that benefits the organization. Tobey (2005) highlights the importance of a training needs assessment as a preliminary process that ensures any applied training is actually supported by organizational needs. It is not enough to simply assume a certain type of training is required. Instead, a training needs assessment will establish that there is a business need that highlights an actual and realized training need. If you do not use a training needs assessment, any training and development initiative may fall flat and could be devoid of general effectiveness.

A training needs assessment done well can really enhance organizational efficiency. For one, it validates training initiatives without assumption. In this regard, training suggestions are rooted in evidence and will hopefully add more value. An effective training needs assessment can also help members of the organization identify legitimate performance gaps.

Ask yourself the following question as you try to identify business needs that may require training.

Questions to Consider

1. What legitimate business problems is the organization experiencing?
2. Are there any concerns about training that need to be addressed early on?
3. What strategic goals are being negatively impacted by the "problem"?
4. What is happening within the organization that is harmful, ineffective, or generally should not occur?
5. What good things are happening within the organization that can be replicated?
6. How might training help solve problems or reinforce good behavior?

PERFORMANCE NEEDS ASSESSMENT

Unlike a training needs assessment, a performance needs assessment tends to focus on a broader organizational perspective. A performance issue can be caused by a lack of training; however, that may not always be the case. In some instances, performance issues may be caused by inadequate resources (i.e., people do not have what they need to perform the job) rather than inadequate skills (i.e., something that may be solved by training). Many times, training may not be the answer. Organizations may have to address performance gaps by increasing motivation and job satisfaction, providing additional resources, or streamlining processes. A performance needs assessment recognizes that there is more to the equation than simply providing training.

Ask yourself the following questions as you try to identify performance gaps that may require solutions.

Questions to Consider

1. Do all employees have what they need to do their jobs effectively?
2. Are there rewards involved when employees do something well or consequences when a job is performed poorly?

3. Are the organizational processes efficient, clear, streamlined, and genuinely useful when trying to achieve the strategic goal?

4. Are performance standards achievable?

5. Is there a feedback loop between the employee(s) and the organization?

ORGANIZATIONAL NEEDS ASSESSMENT

Finally, an organization-wide needs assessment will present an even bigger picture view of the organization as a whole. I believe it is important to distinguish between a performance assessment and something that audits or assesses the organization at large. There may be times when a performance gap exists because the organizational structure is insufficient. For example, there may be "too many bosses," which means that reporting becomes confusing. Or there could be a conflict between the board of trustees and members of the executive leadership team. There may also be a culture issue where the climate is not positive or supportive and employees struggle to complete their tasks because they work in fear or feel disconnected. An organizational needs assessment approaches potential business problems or performance gaps from a more holistic perspective. Organizational structures, leadership, and top-down communication initiatives may be targeted during an organizational needs assessment.

Ask yourself the following questions as you consider organizational challenges.

Questions to Consider

1. What higher order issues is your organization facing (e.g., high turnover, resistant employees, poor leadership, disorganized organizational structure, etc.)?

2. Is the organizational structure supportive of maximum efficiency?

3. Does the organizational culture emphasize a positive or supportive climate?

4. How do leadership and employees interact?

Needs Assessment Evaluation Tools

Your needs assessment is the first step in a successful audit. Before you move to Step 2, data collection and methodology, you must identify holistic organizational needs. If you want to conduct a needs assessment that can help propel your communication audit, use the following evaluative measures to begin your assessment. The following is a checklist of sorts as you move through the needs assessment process.

Stakeholders	Identify who you need to talk to and why.
Methods	Gather preliminary information pertaining to needs through the following: • Surveys • Interviews • Focus Groups • Document analysis • Observations • Literature review
Initial concerns	Start documenting initial concerns you have discovered. Identify any themes and inconsistencies.
Underlying communication issue	Once you have identified initial concerns, is there an underlying communication issue that connects these challenges?

ACTIVITY

Use the checklist below to move forward in your needs assessment process.

_____ Identify potential stakeholders.

_____ Determine tools to gather preliminary information.

_____ Document initial concerns.

_____ Identify any communication themes and inconsistencies.

_____ Identify any underlying communication issues.

Putting It All Together

This chapter was a big picture overview of the purpose of a needs assessment. The needs assessment is a crucial first step in a communication audit.

I recently met with a client, and the procedure looked something like this (through the needs assessment step). Figure 6.2 represents this sequence visually.

- Client makes initial contact requesting a communication audit.

- Initial consult scheduled with client.

- Initial conversation led to a suggestion to bring in other key stakeholders.

- Discovery session held with key stakeholders.

- Organizational scan (including job descriptions, organizational policies and procedures, etc.) related to topics discussed in the initial consult and discovery session conducted.

- Survey developed and distributed throughout the organization that asked employees and leaders about topics revealed during initial consultation/discovery.

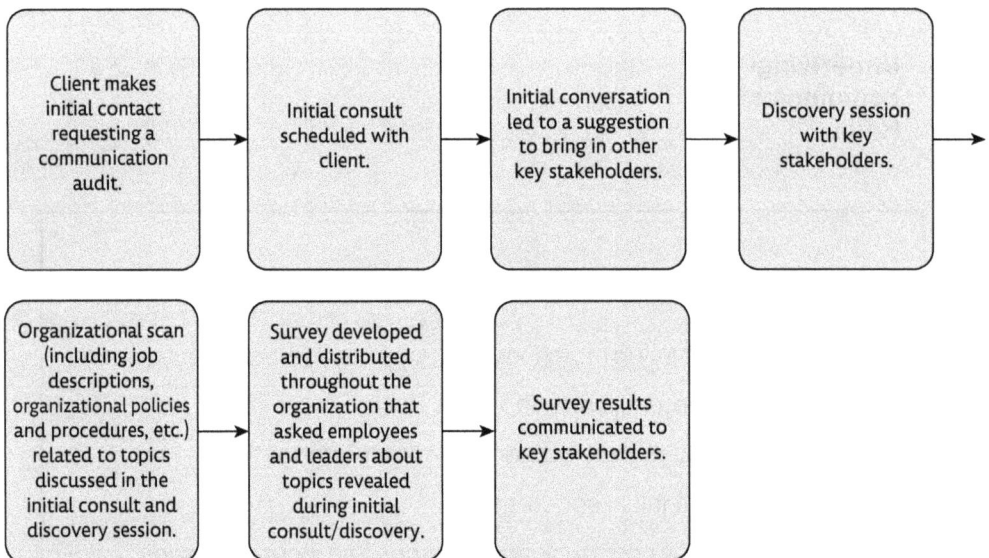

| Figure 6.2 Overview of the Purpose of a Needs Assessment

- Survey results communicated to key stakeholders.

Keep in mind, this progression only led us through the completion of the needs assessment step! Before truly engaging in an in-depth audit, you need to know what potential issues and challenges may be. Do not waste your own time or the organization's. Instead, think strategically about what needs to be evaluated during the audit. You will save time, resources, and angst by identifying and addressing any potential issues early on.

Additional Needs Assessment Resources

Kaufman, R., & Guerra-Lopez, I. (2013). *Needs assessment for organizational success.* American Society for Training and Development. ASTD Press.

Phillips, J., & Holton, III, E. F. (1995). *In action: Conducting needs assessment.* ASTD Press.

Tobey, D. (2005). *Needs assessment basics.* ASTD Press.

Witkin, B. R. (1984). *Assessing needs in educational and social programs: Using information to make decisions, set priorities, and allocate resources.* Jossey-Bass.

ACTIVITIES AND DISCUSSION QUESTIONS

1. Why are needs assessments important?

   _____

   _____

   _____

   _____

   _____

   _____

2. Use the following table to identify pre-assessment, assessment, and post-assessment procedures:

Pre-Assessment	Assessment	Post-Assessment

WHAT WOULD YOU DO?

All of us have been part of an organization, club, team, or group at some point. Think back to a recent involvement where you had some semblance of communication-related conflict. Now imagine you have been asked to analyze the communication efforts of this group and that you have been tasked with conducting a needs assessment. Work through the needs assessment checklist presented in this chapter, providing details below.

_____ Identify potential stakeholders.

_____ Determine tools to gather preliminary information.

_____ Document initial concerns.

_____ Identify any communication themes and inconsistencies.

_____ Identify any underlying communication issues.

_____

_____

_____

_____

_____

_____

_____

_____

_____

_____

_____

_____

_____

CHAPTER 7

The Process, Step 2: Collecting Data and Methodology

This chapter will detail different methodologies for collecting data, including surveys, focus groups, in-depth interviews, and so on. You will be given sample surveys, different communication-specific measurement tools, and other templates that will be helpful when collecting data.

In Chapter 4, we suggested determining the methodologies you will use to collect data: Surveys, focus groups, in-depth interviews, critical incident analyses, network analyses, and observation are all legitimate and potentially necessary data collection methods. These methods will be discussed in depth in this chapter.

Data Collection in Context

The list of collection methods below is not exhaustive, but it is close. The suggestions here are based on traditional research methods. While you may not be conducting the same research as those in an academic community, as the auditor you are still collecting data, and each method has different strengths and weaknesses that can help you reach your strategic audit goals.

SURVEYS

Surveys, otherwise known as questionnaires, can be helpful for collecting data at scale. Practically, questionnaires are efficient, inexpensive, anonymous (if you want them to be), and helpful for collecting data from a large sample size. All employees of large organizations can have a survey distributed to them at minimum monetary and time cost to the consultant and the client. Interviews and focus groups can be extremely time consuming. A survey, especially if you use an instrument that has been created by someone else, is very manageable and can quickly be created and distributed.

If you are developing your own survey, you must be intentional with what you ask and how you ask it. The needs assessment is the central consideration for survey design. If done correctly, you should have identified a focus for assessment based on what you found during the needs assessment. In their work, Downs and Adrian (2004) list important potential topic areas when designing surveys:

- Kinds of information needed to be received and to be sent

- Reactions to sources of information

- Adequacy of channels used

- Relationships among people

- How communication network or structure affects the work processes

- Directions of communication (upward, downward, or horizontal)

- Communication outcomes such as satisfaction and productivity

- Feedback mechanisms and performance

- Communication problem areas

- Interdepartmental communication

- External variables that affect internal communication (p. 107)

This list is a helpful holistic perspective for different ways your survey can address topic areas. Once you have identified a focus, you then need to determine scope, specificity, wording, and relevance for each question.

A self-created survey has certain rules. Downs and Adrian (2004) warn against trying to do too much with individual questions and therefore suggest limiting the scope of different questions and instead asking multiple questions to address one topic area. This leads to their suggestion that questions remain specific; however, you want to avoid being too specific in your questions so as to limit the perspective of the respondent. When designing questions you should also be careful to avoid wording that can be misleading or unhelpful. Avoid biased and insensitive language or language that is confusing. Finally, make sure you include only relevant questions that will help you achieve the audit's goals.

You can use varying question types throughout your survey. Primarily, you will have to choose between open and closed questions. An open question does not restrict an answer (Downs & Adrian, 2004), whereas a closed question is inherently limiting. A closed question will typically give someone a scale, checklist, or ranking system. Open questions will allow the respondent to answer in any capacity they see fit.

Thankfully, there are many premade instruments you can use in surveys or questionnaires. Clampitt (2000) offers several different options, including but not limited to:

- Communication Satisfaction Questionnaire, created by Downs and Haven (1977)

- ICA Audit Survey, created by Goldhaber (1976)

- Organizational Communication Development Audit Questionnaire, created by Wiio (1975)

- Organizational Communication Scale, created by Roberts & O'Reilly (1973)

At the end of this section, I will share a little more about some of my preferred instruments and more specifically resources that will provide background on each scale or measure.

A well-distributed survey will take into consideration several variables. First, consider the number of participants you need to complete the audit goals. Second, consider how the data will be collected and how communication about the survey will be administered. You should describe who you are, discuss the purpose of the audit, share any helpful information related to confidentiality, determine how feedback will be provided to participants, and share any tips for actually completing the survey itself. Before distributing the survey, you should pilot test or run a pretest where you can identify any potential issues.

SURVEY COLLECTION TOOLS AND PLATFORMS

There are several different options for collecting survey data. I typically use a program called Qualtrics or Google Forms. You should research which platform has the capabilities you need and factor cost into your audit proposal. Other highly rated survey platforms include Typeform, Feedier, Survey Monkey, and Alchemer. There are other platforms on the market, so do not settle for one just because it may be cheaper. As you think about a survey collection platform, you want to select something that has an acceptable and aesthetically appealing user interface. I personally prefer platforms that have seamless integration when I do data analysis.

RESEARCH MEASURES

A deep dive into survey methods is beyond the scope of this book. However, if you want to save time and use instruments developed by others to assess organizational efficiency and communication, there are three resources I recommend to you:

Rubin, R. B., Palmgreen, P., & Sypher, H. E. (2004). *Communication research measures: A sourcebook*. Routledge.

Rubin, R. B., Rubin, A. M., Graham, E. E., Perse, E. M., & Seibold, D. R. (2011). *Communication research measures II: A sourcebook*. Routledge.

Graham, E. E., & Mazer, J. (2020). *Communication research measures III: A sourcebook*. Routledge.

These resources contain hundreds of instruments that can be used to measure communication in organizations. These resources are not inexpensive, but their pages house scales and surveys that are reliable and credible and can theoretically be used to collect data on a host of communication issues, including communication satisfaction, communication competence, organizational communication conflict, organizational culture, organizational dissent, and organizational assimilation.

FOCUS GROUPS

Unlike surveys, focus groups can provide in-depth information. As Hamilton (1987) explains, "A focus group is a selection of members of an organization who are interviewed as a group by the communication auditor" (p. 32). Unlike an interview, which only consists of one person, a focus group can be a great resource for gathering ideas that build off one another (Downs & Adrian, 2004). A good auditor recognizes that focus groups and in-depth interviews can be useful to collect information beyond what can be inferred by a survey. Focus groups allow for collective responses to difficult topics. When you select your focus group participants, you want those who are opinion or thought leaders. Typically, you will want diverse representation from the organization, meaning you should look for individuals of varying rank, position, and so on. Generally, you will want your focus group to be no more than five to seven individuals, and when you conduct the session, you may also consider having someone present who can act as a notetaker.

The focus group can provide extremely rich information to the auditor. Dickson (2000) believes a focus group has several characteristics: The topic will be initiated by the moderator (in this case, the auditor); the discussion will usually be recorded; the general purpose is experience-based, meaning the focus group wants to bring to light the experiences of the participants; and the findings will usually be documented in a final report. While surveys are quantitative, where findings are primarily numerical, focus groups are qualitative, allowing the auditor to explore ideas in more depth.

An auditor will use a focus group to capture representation, from the collective, relating to an identified problem or phenomenon. Morgan (1997) highlights three ways an audit can be used to gather information during an audit: as a complementary or subsidiary method or as a stand-alone approach to data collection. By serving as either a complementary or stand-alone resource, focus groups can be invaluable. Downs and Adrian (2004) see seven benefits of focus groups: efficiency, free association, reliability checks, economy, flexibility, speed, and participant satisfaction. They also indicate, though, that the focus group method faces a challenge of realistic interpretation, as comments must be interpreted by the auditor in context to the conversation as a whole. Downs and Adrian also find it hard to generalize due to small sample size, and unlike the interview, a focus group may actually lack depth. Finally, confidentiality and time limit are also considerations to remember if you want to utilize a focus group.

For those who do wish to incorporate focus groups into the audit, remember to control the pace of the group and try to facilitate effectively. You are looking for answers that could not be gained from a survey. Therefore, you want to ask about people's experiences, and you want them to describe in more depth their comments and subsequently have them provide examples or their own thoughts, feelings, and emotions related to something that has happened. The major element here is that you want to have everyone's perspective equally represented.

IN-DEPTH INTERVIEWS

Unlike focus groups, which focus on collective experiences, interviews can be incredible tools for collecting the ideas, opinions, and experiences of the individual. Of the methodologies listed here, surveys/questionnaires, focus groups, and interviews are probably the most common. Like focus groups, interviews can be used as a stand-alone method to collect data or as a wonderful complement to other means. Hamilton (1987) finds that interviews can help clarify an organization's communication structure, reveal job roles and responsibilities, define the organization's values and even the organization's culture, and may provide opportunities for an auditor to identify effects of individual employee personalities, thus drawing connections to potential conflicts. The interview, then, can reveal much about an organization and even relationships therein.

Interviews can provide rich data because of the personal and dyadic nature of the conversation between the interviewer and the interviewee. For one, the interviewer can see and/or hear any inflection or additional information provided by the interviewee that may not be garnered from a quantitative and text-based survey. Even open-ended survey questions cannot provide additional insights into the respondent's emotions. In addition, the interviewer and interviewee can develop a trust and rapport, something that will allow for richer discussion as well as potential follow-up that may not be achieved in other formats. In summary, interviews are exceptionally personal and, if approached correctly, allow for individuals to share in a way that may be therapeutic.

There are, however, potential downfalls to interviews. As Downs and Adrian (2004) discuss, interviews are extremely time consuming and are more difficult to analyze. A survey has a seemingly quick assessment, especially if statistical analyses are needed that are not complicated. Interviews, though, especially taken all together, may be harder to code and therefore make it difficult to decipher different themes.

Practically, interviewers should have an interview guide, something that provides an agenda for the interview and reflects the strategic end goal of the audit. When I create an interview guide, I have the strategic end goal of the audit at the top of the guide. This reminds me to stay focused on the big idea. With that said, you can find a freedom to veer depending on where the conversation is heading, but do not go so far off course that your data does not reflect the purpose(s) of the audit. Additionally, when I create an interview guide, I include specific questions that will help guide our time. If I am conducting an hour-long interview, I usually try to have five to seven questions that need answered. This gives me some flexibility to ask follow-up questions or additional questions that may be a little beyond the current scope.

Before conducting the interview, I try to build rapport with the interviewee by sharing a little about myself and the purpose of the interview. I remind them that I am just there to listen and that this is their chance to share what they may have been holding in as it relates to our discussion about their workplace. I also try to share a little about the audit as a whole. As the interviewer, you will want to share any information you can about the format of the interview and why this individual was selected to participate. Like survey/questionnaire or focus group participants, you want your interview participants to be a representative sample. As you go through the interview, remember to ask primarily open-ended questions that do not reflect your opinion or biases, and assure participants of confidentiality when you can.

Interview questions should be exploratory. You will want to, generally, ask people about their job (role, responsibilities, etc.), the information they need to do their job effectively, strengths/weaknesses of the organization, formal/informal channels of communication, and their ideas for suggestions or improvements to the overall communication flow of their organization (Millar & Gallagher, 2000). As the interviewer, you want to be an objective, nonjudgmental voice and an efficient facilitator (Hamilton, 1987). All told, if done correctly, interviews provide incredibly rich data for a communication audit.

CRITICAL INCIDENT ANALYSIS

A critical incident analysis can take the form of a survey, focus group, or interview, but the data you are collecting tend to be more specific. In a critical incident analysis, participants are asked very specifically to describe effective or ineffective communication experiences at their organization. The purpose is to collect these experiences to then determine what to model in the future. The emphasis is on specific situations, not communication as a whole. The focus is still on the experience(s) of the individual but within a predetermined, specific context. The end goal for a critical incident analysis is reflection. The auditor, in this case, may be brought in to determine why a specific communication event was or was not successful and then make recommendations about what to do if a similar event occurs in the future. While not always the case, a crisis event may necessitate a critical incident analysis.

As you consider using a critical incident analysis, you may want to think about the method from a data collection perspective. The goal here is to have participants recall and describe when a behavior, action, or occurrence impacted (can be either a positive or negative impact) a communication outcome. A critical incident or event should be something that led to a reassessment of individual or organizational learning, and while the event does not need to be earth-shattering, there is an assumption that it is significant. Serrat (2017) reinforces the importance of organizational learning amidst significant events. The process is one of description (what happened), feelings (what they were thinking), evaluation (what was good or bad about the experience), analysis (what sense they can make of the situation), conclusion (what else could have been done), and action plan (if the issue arose again, what they would do differently; Serrat, 2017). This cycle, then, establishes the significant event and the subsequent successful or unsuccessful reactions as distinctive and necessary.

Organizations may be able to assess significant or critical incidents without the help of an external consultant. No matter who is involved, the goal of collecting data surrounding a critical incident is to determine what to do if the same situation happens again.

NETWORK ANALYSIS

A critical event analysis tends to focus on one isolated event, while a network analysis will instead seek to understand the entire communication flow or framework of an organization. For our purposes, during a network analysis, an auditor will holistically explore connections between communication platforms, channels, and how information is exchanged. A network analysis can be a great tool because it potentially reveals immediate barriers or obstacles to communication effectiveness. Without going too deeply, before conducting a network analysis, the auditor must understand what constitutes the network. Who are the people and the connections that need to be analyzed throughout this collection?

A network analysis should be used when the issues are far reaching and may be tied to individual technologies or platforms. Of the methods here, I use network analysis the least, but that does not mean it is not valuable. If you are interested in the structure of the organization as a whole and the actual flow of communication across a widespread connected network, then the network analysis can be an incredibly useful supplementary methodology.

OBSERVATION

Throughout the audit process, you may have to rely on observation as a method of collecting data that may not be accessible through other means. Through observation, empirical data is still collected by human, mechanical, electrical, or electronic means (Erikkson & Kvalainen, 2008). There are four different observation methods described by Erikkson and Kvalainen (2008):

> First, participant and non-participant observation, depending on whether the researcher is part of the situation they are studying or not. Obtrusive and non-obtrusive, or disguised and non-disguised observation, depending on whether the participants know that they are being observed or not. Observation in natural and contrived settings, depending on

whether action is observed where it is occurring "naturally" or in a contrived setting. And structured and non-structured observation, depending on whether a checklist determines what is being observed, or not. (p. 86)

Observation can help the auditor see firsthand different situations that through surveys/questionnaires, focus groups, or interviews may only be described afterward. You may decide to observe several different facets of the organization, but primarily, you want to focus on observing actions and actual happenings, behavior, verbal and nonverbal communication, as well as what may not happen, such as how someone may or may not respond or information that was not relayed (Erikkson & Kvalainen, 2008). As you observe, consider who is involved, what event is occurring and who was the primary initiator, how participants react, and what happens after the interaction is finished. Remember, also, that data collected should be confidential and you should protect the identity of those you observe so they can feel free to act naturally.

An astute auditor will want to observe if given the opportunity. Like document review and content analysis, observation can give you incredible firsthand organizational insight. This can give you a valuable perspective when collecting additional data and completing the final report. As a matter of preference—but also what I would argue is best practice—I like to inform organizations that I may be observing on different occasions. I prefer the observational elements to not be a surprise for ethical reasons. This prior knowledge of the visit may lead to some in the organization "putting on airs," but observing for several hours or days will still provide wonderful context for the audit.

DOCUMENT REVIEW

Your role as an auditor will probably involve collecting new data. However, you must also review past strategic or communication plans and find valuable information embedded within these documents. You have to make yourself familiar with past assessments, audits, and strategies if you want to find out where previous plans have failed. A document review (otherwise known as a content analysis) focuses on organizational records kept by the organization (Hamilton, 1987). Anything (relevant to the audit) that is documented and recorded should be analyzed by the auditor as part of the process. Typically, I conduct a document review at the beginning of the process. This allows me to craft my needs assessment and subsequent surveys, interviews, and so on with purpose and intentionality. It also gives me a breadth of organizational knowledge. However, I have found that I need to sometimes revisit a content analysis throughout the audit.

Like all other data collection methods, the content analysis should be conducted in an objective manner. Hamilton (1987) reiterates that the "secret to an effective content analysis is the selection of what has to be counted and measured" (p. 82). Hamilton further suggests different categories to use to classify documentation: by subject at issue (e.g., personnel, administrative practices, planning, etc.), by type of communication, by source, by destination, and by action taken. These categories are extremely helpful because of the inherent focus on communication. As such, your analysis of these documents should focus on the appropriateness, the frequency, and clarity and style of the document examined.

The data you analyze at the content analysis step should be representative of the organization as a whole. Like Hamilton (1987) goes on to say, you want to identify 80% of what goes on at an organization by examining 20% of their documentation. The content you collect can be almost anything, so choose selectively. The content you select should be diverse but representative. After you have content and documents to analyze, you will still have to establish a coding scheme to identify big picture themes.

Putting It All Together

The methods listed here can help you gather data to then make recommendations and suggestions. The next chapter will discuss how to analyze these methodologies and what to notice and share as results. Table 7.1 lists each method discussed, along with the benefits, challenges, cost, time commitment, and type of data collected.

TABLE 7.1   Data Collection Table

Method	Benefits	Challenges	Cost (high, medium, or low)	Time	Data collected
Survey	Efficient, not as expensive as interviews or focus groups, anonymous and confidential	Surface-level information	Medium	Depends on survey length and whether or not you are developing the instrument	Quantitative
Focus group	Deep and rich information, ideas build off one another, collective responses to difficult topics	A potential for groupthink, confidentiality concerns, must have representative sample	High	Can be extremely time consuming depending on number of participants	Qualitative
In-depth interview	Deep and rich information, in-depth responses to difficult topics, can be a stand-alone method	Tendency to potentially get off track of main topic, confidentiality concerns, must have representative sample	High	Can be extremely time consuming depending on number of participants	Qualitative
Network analysis	Entire organization analyzed and connections therein	May be difficult to ascertain what data to collect and how, must demonstrate impact and connection	Medium	Depending on outcomes, can be time consuming if exhaustive	Quantitative

Observation	Provides auditor context and has organizational knowledge	May cloud the judgement of the auditor	Low	May be minimal	Qualitative
Document review	Offers historical knowledge of organization that is valuable for making connections	Hard to determine what materials to include in the review	Low	Could be substantial, depending on number of artifacts	Qualitative

Additional Data Collection and Methodology Resources

Boyle, M. P., & Schmierbach, M. (2015). *Applied communication research methods: Getting started as a researcher.* Routledge.

Bradburn, N., Sudman, S., & Wansink, B. (2004). *Asking questions: The definitive guide to questionnaire design for market research, political polls, and social and health questionnaires.* Jossey-Bass.

Dillman, D. A., Smyth, J. D., & Christian, L. M. (2009). *Internet, mail, and mixed-mode surveys: The tailored design method* (3rd ed.). John Wiley & Sons.

Rubin, R. B., Rubin, A. M., Haridakis, P. M., & Piele, L. J. (2010). *Communication research strategies and sources* (7th ed.). Wadsworth Cengage Learning.

ACTIVITIES AND DISCUSSION QUESTIONS

1. In your own words, describe the following data collection techniques:

Method	Definition
Survey	
Focus group	
In-depth interview	

Method		
Network analysis		
Observation		
Document review		

2. In your own words, describe the benefits and challenges of each approach:

Method	Benefits	Challenges
Survey		
Focus group		
In-depth interview		
Network analysis		
Observation		
Document review		

WHAT WOULD YOU DO?

Imagine you have been asked to conduct a communication audit where you are trying to identify why employees seem to be ignoring emails from supervisors. Without knowing any additional information at this point, which data collection techniques may be most appropriate, and why?

_____

_____

_____

_____

_____

_____

_____

_____

_____

_____

_____

_____

CHAPTER 8

The Process, Step 3: Analyzing Data and Clarifying Results

T his chapter will serve as an overview of analyzing data and looking for common themes or indicators of ineffective communication. You will be given a crash course in finding relevant communication data.

Surveys

As mentioned in Chapter 7, surveys can be extremely effective for gathering data at scale and quantifying perspectives. The key feature of surveys is the ability to determine connections between different elements you are interested in. For example, you may want to know if there is a connection between employee satisfaction and communication competence. Surveys can provide information related to how those variables connect. Surveys can also help you understand long-term trends. In this way, surveys can be longitudinal, and you can collect data at different intervals to measure any change that has occurred.

Analyzing Quantitative Data

There are several ways to analyze quantitative data. For the sake of simplicity, Clampitt (2000) describes three basic methods for data analysis:

- **Rank-order method:** This method has a high reliance on question means. When you ask a question and get a response, the mean is the average score achieved. So in this case you would use the "means from each question and simply 'rank' related items from high to low" (p. 60).

- **Databank comparisons:** If a databank (composed of results from other distributions of a survey) exists, then you can compare the results from your audit to those that have been identified in previous studies.

- **Factor score:** Audits may reveal key factors or groupings of questions that reveal underlying issues. Factor scores allow you to see key relationships between variables.

Statistical Analyses

It is important to remember that doing statistical analysis using programs can require years of training, but with some available resources, one can do more simple forms of analysis. Thankfully, electronic surveys have many benefits compared to the historical pen-and-paper method. For our purposes, electronic surveys allow for user-friendly data analysis. Most programs, like Qualtrics (mentioned in Chapter 7), will have an embedded algorithm that will allow you to see and make connections between survey variables. There may be times, though, when you have to conduct analyses yourself or when you must incorporate your data into a different program (like SPSS, a software program specifically designed for data analysis). In this case, you must determine which analyses to consider:

- **Regression tests:** used to determine cause and effect relationships. Example tests include simple linear regression, multiple linear regression, and logistic regression.

- **Comparison tests:** look for differences among group means (i.e., group average scores). Example tests include paired t-test, independent t-test, ANOVA, and MANCOVA.

- **Correlation tests:** check whether two variables are related without assuming a cause-and-effect relationship. Examples include a Pearson's r test.

Generally, you will not have to conduct these tests yourself. What is important here is the understanding that through quantitative data, you can determine cause and effect relationships, differences among groups, and variable relationships. If you are interested, here are several resources available that can help provide insight into statistical analyses:

Anderson, A. (2013). *Business statistics for dummies*. Wiley.

Hargie, O., & Tourish, D. (2000). *Handbook of communication audits for organizations*. Routledge.

James, G., Witten, D., Hastie, T., & Tibshirani, R. (2013). *An introduction to statistical learning with applications in R.* (2nd ed.) Springer.

Theobald, O. (2020). *Statistics for absolute beginners* (2nd ed.). Scatterplot Press.

Wheelan, C. (2014). *Naked statistics: Stripping the dread from the data*. Norton.

Focus Groups

Focus groups and interviews represent similar qualitative data sources. Qualitative data, put simply, is nonnumerical data that characterizes or defines. This type of data can be observed (which will be discussed below) or recorded, as many focus groups and interviews tend to be. You can collect qualitative data through questionnaires or surveys by employing open-ended questions. Focus groups are those individuals who are brought together purposefully by the auditor to discuss the issue at hand. Eriksson and Kovalainen (2008) provide a wonderful method for focus group analysis. The questions they offer provide great initial ideas for analyzing focus group data and determining themes:

Questions to Consider

1. Did several participants repeat the issue or make similar statements about the issue?

2. Did several participants remain silent on an issue or disagree about a particular issue?

3. Did participants across groups (if there are multiple groups) repeat the issue or make similar statements about the issue?

4. Did the issue of agreement/disagreement about the issue have unusual importance to the participants demonstrated by either verbal or nonverbal communication?

5. How intensely did the participants state their views about the issue?
6. Did anyone change their point of view about the issue in a significant way?
7. What clues do you have concerning the reasons for a change in discussion?
8. What was the context of the conversation when something interesting happened?
9. What was the whole conversation like as a process?

As you analyze focus group data, you should be concerned with what is said, how it is said, and, most specifically, how the group interacts when discussing certain topics. You should record the interaction if you can: Video is sometimes more helpful because you can go back and review nonverbal distinctions. You also need to take copious notes during the focus group to help you stay focused and review your own thoughts later on in the process.

If you can, engage in preliminary analysis as soon as possible after the focus group concludes. This keeps data fresh in your mind. You should try to interpret and explain what you observed through the group discussion.

General analysis of the focus group content should focus on different themes and patterns that were revealed during the discussion. As such, you need to perform a content analysis. To do content analysis of focus group data, identify statements that are common with group members, then use quotations to reinforce your findings. When it comes to focus group data, you must be selective about what you report and how you report it. Highlight those quotations that are most relevant to the audit at hand.

In-Depth Interviews

Like focus groups, interviews are also a supported qualitative method. Interviews are a focused discussion. Typically, in both focus groups and interviews, a list of predetermined questions is identified, but the conversation should not be so structured that you cannot ask follow-up questions. Interviews are dyadic, consisting of the interviewer and the interviewee.

Interviews have a different ethos, depending on the focus. Eriksson and Kovalainen (2008) identify three different types of interviews: positivist (interested in facts), emotionalist (interested in how people experience the issue in question), and constructivist (interested in how meanings are produced during the actual interview interaction). As part of the interview process, the interviewer should observe participant behavior (more on this below). Like focus groups, as you analyze data from interviews, you should focus on themes that are present throughout the individual interview and also connected through multiple interviews. Interviews can also be analyzed using a narrative approach where you make sense of a connection between individual interviewee's stories. These two analysis methods, content analysis and narrative analysis, are inductive. In this case, the data speaks for itself, and themes emerge through the data collection process. You may, however, conduct a deductive analysis where you, the facilitator and analyzer, will have different themes you believe exist, and then you would connect interview data to these predetermined categories. In some cases this can evolve after the in-depth needs assessment process.

Critical Incident Analysis

The critical incident analysis process is primarily focused on identifying key factors associated with personal narratives connected to an isolated event. Auditors who engage in a critical incident analysis should have access to personal experiences told by those in an organization. Holistically, then, you are concerned about personal narratives of the participants or key players (Alanazi, 2018). Your primary concern is to identify key influential factors that led to either a successful or unsuccessful result.

Participants during a critical incident analysis should remember when something (like a behavior, action, or occurrence) influenced or impacted an outcome. Before engaging in a critical incident analysis, you must be sure that there was a cause-and-effect relationship between the incident and the outcome. While a critical incident analysis is most commonly used during interviews, you can also ask critical questions during focus groups or surveys. Unlike a general question—or even one that is extremely open ended—a critical analysis question asks about a specific incident and how that incident was instrumental to the accomplishment of a task. When you ask questions, you can separately ask both positive and negative variations.

Like interviews and focus groups, you should think about the data primarily in terms of categories or themes. For a critical incident analysis, it is important to think about relevance and credibility, especially because you are relying so much on personal narratives. This is why going back and reviewing audio or video recordings is crucial. You should review the discussions until no new themes are discovered, meaning you have reached a saturation point. As you consider the validity of claims, there should be agreement surrounding the critical analysis, and you should be able to ask respondents to cross-check the validity of the incident proclamations. When you review the data, take specific interest in the cause, outcome, and description of the critical event as well as individual feelings and perceptions of the situation. Most importantly, you should identify actions taken during the incident and then any changes in future behavior that positively or negatively impacted the event.

Network Analysis

A network is a collection of elements that are interconnected. In our case, as you can imagine, we are concerned most about technological connections; something that deals primarily with communication and communication platforms; social connections; or relationships between coworkers. As well as information connections, specifically identifying information flow through the network.

You have a few options when analyzing network data. We are blending into communicating results, but you can produce a visualization of a complex system and literally visually represent the network connections. However, there are steps to take before it is time to show results.

A network analysis can be used to describe relationships among individuals or units in organizations. From a communications perspective, networks represent who communicates. As you look at relationships in organizations, you should see connections at both an individual (focusing on personal attributes) or organizational (understanding who is the authority on certain topics) level. You should be concerned, then, with two primary variables: relational, which are those created from direct ties (e.g., connectedness, group membership, etc.) and structural, which are those created from the entire network (e.g., position).

There are five major network data collection techniques, which Hayes et al. (2008) suggest are survey, egocentric (measuring a person's connections or friends), snowball (interviewing a random selection of individuals), census (asking for nominations of network members), or joint (nominations of events or organizational memberships).

There are three levels of analysis for networks. These dimensions function as categorizations. The three levels are individual (including personal network density or central individuals), group (group formation based on direct ties or hierarchical position), and network (dense or sparse networks as well as centralization of positions). A network analysis measures network connections at these three levels, and for the sake of simplicity, a network analysis does measure who communicates and how.

I have used modified network analyses in communication audits. These can be helpful for identifying relationships and communication barriers and especially for highlighting and inventorying different communication platforms. I highly recommend Hayes et al.'s (2008) resource in *The SAGE Sourcebook of Advanced Data Analysis Methods for Communication Research*.

Observation

As an auditor, observation can be a wonderful supplement to the overall process. As the communication expert, you can study how relationships form and develop and how information flows in an organization. As you analyze your observation data, consider a few key components:

Questions to Consider

1. Who are the major stakeholders, and more importantly, who is actively initiating communication?

2. What themes have you noticed that arise during day-to-day office interactions?

3. How are individuals reacting to different supervisors, coworkers, or even to varying messages?

4. At the nonverbal level, who do people look at when certain topics arise?

The important consideration here is that the data you find during your observations will help you shed light on other findings. When reflecting on what I have observed in organizations, it is important to think about consistency. If your observations seem out of place with what you are finding through surveys, interviews, or focus groups, then there is probably something amiss, and there is a potential that people are not being honest through the other assessment means. With that said, it is a great sign if your observation data reinforces what you are seeing and hearing through other data collection means.

Document Review

Throughout a document review, you will primarily be using a content analysis framework. A content analysis can focus on themes or categories, just like interviews and focus groups, but you can also be a little more quantitative and record word or phrase frequencies and calculate how often different expressions or words are discovered.

A document review presents an opportunity to also consider inefficiencies (or, more positively, things that are going well). In this regard, a document review may be a helpful supplement to a network analysis, and you may consider using a content map to diagram how different tools/platforms, relationships, or opinions connect throughout the organization. A document review can also be useful for a chronological perspective, as you can diagram different policies or procedures over time. Existing or historical documents provide insight that transcends current employees.

In addition to serving as a historical perspective, analyzing appropriate documents can also help you understand philosophical underpinnings in organizations. Also, if you are conducting a communication audit for the purposes of initiating new training, you can (hopefully) go back and review previous training evaluations and see how similar programs fared in the past.

As you analyze documents, searching again for themes, categories, and connections to other data and the organization at large, you may need to also communicate with those in the organization with substantial organizational knowledge. Find those who were around initially when the document was in use or created. Document review, as a relatively inexpensive means of assessment, can provide wonderful background information and may show concerns not unearthed by other means.

ACTIVITIES AND DISCUSSION QUESTIONS

1. Research some potential quantitative data analysis tools that are user friendly and cost-effective or free.

   _____

   _____

   _____

   _____

   _____

   _____

2. In your own words, describe what you are looking for when you try to identify themes in qualitative data.

   _____

   _____

   _____

   _____

   _____

   _____

3. What clarifying questions do you have about data collection or analysis? What confuses you at this point?

_____

_____

_____

_____

_____

_____

_____

_____

_____

_____

WHAT WOULD YOU DO?

Imagine you launched a survey addressing communication satisfaction, and 350 employee responses have been returned to you. Your survey was a mix of closed and open-ended questions. You want to start analyzing the data. What should be your first step, and how would you start the process of analyzing such a high volume of responses?

_____

_____

_____

_____

_____

CHAPTER 9

The Process, Step 4: Communicating the Results

T his chapter will help you think about communicating the results of your audit. You will be directed to find strategic or key indicators and then communicate those indicators clearly to varying stakeholders.

After you have conducted your needs assessment, collected data, and then analyzed the results, it is now time to communicate your findings to the organization. This is an integral step in the audit process and is something that cannot be ignored. It is, unfortunately, not as simple as just affirming different key themes or phrases or even numerical findings. Instead, there is an embedded psychology when you share your audit revelations. I believe there are 10 key steps to accomplish when you communicate your results, as outlined in Figure 9.1.

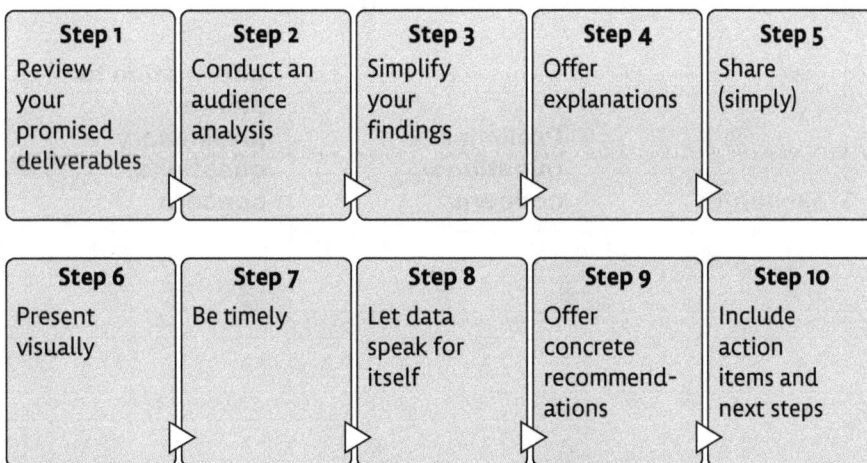

Step 1	**Step 2**	**Step 3**	**Step 4**	**Step 5**
Review your promised deliverables	Conduct an audience analysis	Simplify your findings	Offer explanations	Share (simply)

Step 6	**Step 7**	**Step 8**	**Step 9**	**Step 10**
Present visually	Be timely	Let data speak for itself	Offer concrete recommend-ations	Include action items and next steps

| Figure 9.1 The 10 Key Steps to Communicating Audit Results

Before we dive deeper into each step, let's first consider stakeholder communication.

Stakeholder Communication

Generally speaking, you should be privy to the key stakeholders by the time your audit is completed. If you do not know who is crucial in the decision-making process, then a step has been missed. However, assuming you do know your stakeholders, you should be documenting, literally or figuratively, what they care about. As such, when you get to this step of communicating the results of your findings, you can think very specifically about what each stakeholder or stakeholder group needs to know.

Audits differ drastically in their stakeholder conceptions. As discussed earlier in the text, you may have to share findings with supervisors/managers, the organization at large, a board of trustees, and so on. In some regard, the combination of stakeholder potential is seemingly endless. With that said, you should revisit your initial notes from preliminary meetings to clearly articulate, yet again, what each group or individual needs to know.

Table 9.1 will help you again identify your key stakeholders, revisit what they initially cared about in the first place, and then summarize your findings based on their preliminary concerns.

TABLE 9.1   Stakeholder Communication

Stakeholder	Preliminary questions/ concern	Information to answer preliminary questions/ concern

Clearly aligning the stakeholder with their desired end and then using your audit processes/data to meet their concern will provide direct and immediate value for each stakeholder group. I would recommend completing some variation of this table before you consider communicating your results in any fashion.

As you reflect on each stakeholder, consider, yet again, your communication objectives. What are you trying to convey, what is your main or primary message for each group, and how will the evidence you provide reinforce this key message? These are crucial considerations for you to think about before launching into a full-fledged consideration of stakeholder communication. The steps below will highlight different ways you can adhere to stakeholder desires as you communicate the results of your findings.

STEP 1:
REVIEW YOUR PROMISED DELIVERABLES

Remember that the audit process is a process, a procedure. As such, at this point you need to go back to the very beginning and review notes and observations from initial meetings. Specifically, at this step you need to find what you promised the stakeholders before you finalized a contract or a memorandum of understanding. In your initial conversations you should have identified different deliverables that you would be sure to provide at the end of the audit. This is your chance to make sure that you are clearly providing everything you said you would.

Generally, when engaging in an audit, you will probably include a final report as one of the, if not the sole, deliverables. As you consider this final report, make sure you align the format of the report with promised expectations. The main idea: Deliver on what you promised and communicate what you said you would provide.

Questions to Consider

1. Did you specify that the report would be accessible to all members of the organization or just executive or key leadership?

2. Did your deliverables include a virtual report or one presented face to face?

3. Did you specify that you would provide a full detailed report or an executive summary?

STEP 2:
CONDUCT AN AUDIENCE ANALYSIS

While you should have a well-established working relationship with organizational stakeholders, you may be communicating results to those who you have not interacted with on a regular basis. At this point, then, it is suggested that you complete an audience analysis.

In the world of public speaking, an audience analysis consists primarily of identifying the audience and adapting your presentation to their knowledge level, attitudes, and even beliefs about a certain topic. Delivering the results of an audit puts you in a different situation. You cannot hide difficult findings (more on that in the next chapter), and more importantly, you have been paid, hopefully, to provide true and relevant insight. So tailoring what you present to your audience becomes difficult.

Analyzing an audience can be accomplished in several ways. You can consider their demographics, their knowledge of the organization and even the knowledge of your audit, your relationship with the audience as a whole, and even their expectations. Generally, results should speak to the interest of the listener. This means you, as the presenter, need to tailor your message so that your information is primarily relevant to the hearer. Most stakeholders will be invested, if not heavily invested, in your audit, but they will primarily want to know what is most applicable to them, their department, and what they oversee. As you work with your initial point of contact to discuss who will be on the receiving end of your results-oriented message, make sure you document interests and try to design your report accordingly.

STEP 3:
SIMPLIFY YOUR FINDINGS

The key to communication is clarity. Your primary objective as you communicate your findings should be simplicity. You may have discovered results that require higher order thinking or a deep knowledge of data analysis. However, part of your role is to take those complicated findings and make them digestible for any stakeholder with any type of knowledge. As you present, you will want to be open and honest where appropriate. Your level of transparency will usually be determined by your audience. Make sure that you and your point of contact have explored what is and is not appropriate for each group prior to sharing your results.

Questions to Consider

1. What major themes did you find?
2. What key components or contributions are central to this discussion?
3. How do your results connect to initial questions posted during preliminary conversations?

As you consider your results, remember to consider the big picture. How do your results fit into the broader organizational context? While considering this broader organizational context, highlight your key findings and be prepared to challenge conventional assumptions from the group based on your data.

STEP 4:
OFFER EXPLANATIONS

When appropriate, you should offer explanations of data if findings seem to be inconsistent. Be prepared to offer an overview of your data collection methodologies, potentially highlighting why you decided to do, for instance, focus groups instead of interviews. Articulating the purpose behind your chosen methods may help stave off any potential issues or inconsistencies. With that said, there may be times where you genuinely (a) see that the data does not align or (b) believe something is missing from the data. In these instances, you should be prepared to offer an explanation. Typically, I want to be prepared to address inconsistencies but may not directly bring up concerns like this to a general group. For example, if an organization-wide survey reveals high employee satisfaction but focus groups consistently reveal consternation or dissatisfaction, you should be prepared to address this finding. Depending on who I am speaking with and the context, I may share these inconsistencies as part of a general report, but I will want to do so judiciously. Remember here, you are the subject matter expert, and in this case, you are the data expert. You have an intimate relationship with your findings that the audience will not have. As such, you are the translator. It is up to you to determine what needs to be shared and when. Finally, it is also important to note that when you offer findings, you should do so in a way that protects the audit participants and the organization at large from reprisal.

STEP 5:
SHARE (SIMPLY)

Sharing your results with simplicity is tied intimately to simplifying your findings. However, there are a few key considerations that you need to remember as you actually go through the process of sharing your results. First, you want to make sure that you move from high-order results, or high-level results, to those that would be considered lower level. Present the big picture first before allowing your audience to fall through the cracks. You must present the higher level results to then move to the more detailed findings. Second, you probably want to, and need to, get more into the weeds with key leadership. While you can usually share general results with larger groups, key executive team members will want to know details. This is where you can share individual comments from participants or more vulnerable themes. Third, you may want to consider sharing department- or team-specific results with those who participate in those groups. For example, ff you are finding substantial data related to human resources, then you should clarify those findings and share appropriately.

From a practical perspective, there are different steps you can take to communicate your findings simply. For one, structure your content in a logical way. This is why moving from high-level to low-level findings is helpful. There should be an embedded structure to your presentation or report. If the content seems cumbersome, consider breaking it up or chunking it into smaller sections. From a formatting perspective, headings in a formal report or transitional phrases in a presentation can help your audience move from point to point seamlessly.

Your content should also be presented in plain and jargon-free language. Leave out details that are not needed or distracting, and be satisfied with presenting important information first before moving on to less urgent considerations. You should be conversational, clear, and direct. Be active in your vocal demonstrations, not passive, and use language your audience will understand. You are allowed to be excited about your content; in fact, animation and charisma can help your overall effectiveness, but do not allow your enthusiasm to cloud the results.

You should also be purposefully repetitive: Consider how you can present content and key ideas in multiple ways. Generally, be concise, be helpful, and be clear.

STEP 6:
PRESENT VISUALLY

I do not consider myself to be creative when it comes to designing anything aesthetic. However, I have found that presenting my findings visually, when I can, helps the audience see unique results that they may miss when just relayed via spoken or written word. Presenting your results visually can really bring the results to life. There are a number of different ways to present findings visually and several platforms you can use to create aesthetically appealing materials. With that said, I consistently use Canva (www.canva.com) to create visually stimulating resources for my clients. Canva has a number of free templates, and they have a free version that I have found to be appropriate for my needs. Prezi, a more visual version of PowerPoint, can also be helpful if used effectively. When visually representing your data, remember that less can often be more. You should not overwhelm your audience with visuals or make visuals too "busy" and confusing. Simplicity and clarity still apply when using graphs, charts, or infographics to highlight findings.

A few quick tips are helpful for creating presentations that incorporate a visual data representation:

- Keep data simple and use simple data presentation tools.

- Label all charts, graphs, figures, or tables.

- Use a similar aesthetic throughout to allow for accessible comparison.

- Make everything easy to read and understand.

- Do not overload with color or graphics.

- Make sure you do not overwhelm your audience with information.

- Limit the amount of information, especially words, on your slides if you are using a slide deck to present information.

If this interests you, you should consider additional exploration of data visualization. It is a fascinating area of study and something that is needed more every day.

STEP 7:
BE TIMELY

Theoretically, all of your results will be presented when the client needs or wants them. However, you can serve your client well by presenting urgent results as soon as you can. If you find issues that are pressing and of genuine concern, those should be presented and shared in a timely manner. With that said, all of your results should be presented while the client can still make good decisions regarding future actions. When you communicate your results, be diligent to stick to the time frame that was promised during the initial meetings.

As important, timely communication of results also relates to the amount of time needed to share results. Do not be too long winded in your delivery. Be concise, be relevant, and be applicable. Respect the time of your clients, and present information when and where it works for them.

STEP 8:
LET DATA SPEAK FOR ITSELF

As an auditor, and as one who would usually be in a consulting role, you may be tempted to insert your own opinions based on sheer observation and experience. Communicating your results means exactly that: Present what you have discovered throughout the process. If you have followed the steps and collected data in a manner that is both valid and reliable, then your results should speak for themselves. The data you collected should serve as the primary means by which you offer your results and recommendations. You need not contrive different opinions. Your credibility as a consultant will be further enhanced by presenting your findings as a solid foundation and baseline for your recommendations.

STEP 9:
OFFER CONCRETE RECOMMENDATIONS

When you allow your data to speak for itself, you can offer suggestions and recommendations based on your findings, not just your hunches. You should communicate your findings in such a way that there is a seamless transition to concrete recommendations. Your recommendations should be tangible and presented in a way that brings to light the data and offers a path to quantifiable impact on the business and the communication avenues of the business or organization. Your recommendations should be presented in a manner that connects your data with the recommendations. Thus, framing your recommendations as "Our data indicates _____. Therefore, you have the following options for making changes: _____" can be helpful as a mechanism to show the holistic framework. If there is one identifiable concrete recommendation, then present that information accordingly. However, because you are the auditor and not the primary decision maker, you should present multiple alternatives and options when appropriate. By this time, you probably have intimate knowledge of the organization's strategic plan. By aligning your recommendations with strategic goals, you can help the client think deeply about their subsequent action steps.

STEP 10:
INCLUDE ACTION ITEMS AND NEXT STEPS

Concrete recommendations may be different from actual action steps or even immediate next steps that the organization must take. A recommendation is usually strategic; there is some underlying longer term implication. An immediate action step or immediate next step tends to be, as you can imagine, short term in nature. In other words, what can be done right away to make a change? Again, based on your findings, you should be prepared to offer suggestions to the stakeholders about what can be quickly accomplished to help achieve big picture goals. The immediate next steps may include additional data collection, further conversations, or even immediate training. No matter what you suggest, both in terms of concrete recommendations and immediate action items, clearly tie your recommendations to your results.

Putting It All Together

The audit process can be a long and drawn-out experience for both you and your client. The steps identified here, from conducting a needs assessment, to identifying measures you will use to collect data, analyzing data, and finally communicating results, hopefully establish clarity in terms of what the auditor should accomplish. When you conduct a communication audit, you are trying to pinpoint communication problems through data collection and then offer recommendations based on your findings and expertise. The process identified here has significant implications for determining how organizations are or are not communicating effectively and what can be accomplished to help establish true communication clarity, solid information flow, and enhance relationships across the organization.

Additional Resources on Results Communication

Tufte, E. (2011). *The visual display of quantitative information* (2nd ed.). Graphics Press.

Williams, R. (2014). *The non-designers design book* (4th ed.). Peachpit Press.

ACTIVITIES AND DISCUSSION QUESTIONS

Use the following template to outline your preliminary results presentation.

Introduction:

_____

_____

_____

_____

Transition:

_____

_____

_____

_____

_____

Main Point 1:

_____

_____

_____

_____

_____

Items to support or visually represent Main Point 1:

_____

_____

_____

_____

_____

_____

Main Point 2:

_____

_____

_____

_____

_____

Items to support or visually represent Main Point 2:

_____

_____

_____

_____

_____

_____

Main Point 3:

_____

_____

_____

_____

_____

_____

Items to support or visually represent Main Point 3:

_____

_____

_____

_____

_____

_____

Conclusion and Action Steps:

_____

_____

_____

_____

_____

_____

WHAT WOULD YOU DO?

You have been assigned to complete an internal communication audit at your organization. Through preliminary focus groups, you have determined that there is a widespread issue with top–down communication and a lack of trust in employees for their supervisors. Go through the 10 steps presented in this chapter for communicating results. In this particular instance, how could you let the data speak for itself in a situation that may be particularly difficult?

_____

_____

_____

_____

_____

_____

_____

_____

_____

_____

_____

_____

_____

_____

_____

_____

_____

_____

PART III

Practical Applications

CHAPTER 10

Dealing With Results

This chapter will address dealing with overarching, specifically negative, results that may have to deal with conflict management or holistic organizational issues.

Reporting Unfavorable Results

While we would like to assume that every audit is a seamless endeavor, this is, of course, not the case. In fact, probably more often than not you will have to report results to your stakeholders that are not encouraging. This does not mean that the results are incorrect, although they may be, but rather that the news that needs to be shared is not what the stakeholders want to hear. If this is true, the auditor must rely even more substantially on the actual data and use the results of the audit to speak for themselves.

The following sections will help auditors consider what to do when the audit goes wrong or how to communicate, effectively, results that are unfavorable. Specifically, this chapter will explore two different phenomena: What do we do if the audit goes wrong (primarily because of the auditor), and what do we do if our results will frustrate the stakeholders?

Audit Challenges

WHEN THE AUDIT GOES WRONG

First, what do we do when the audit goes wrong? Tobey (2005) identifies a few common errors when conducting a needs assessment, and I believe these same issues can be present in a communication audit:

- Insufficient data collection or analysis

- Treating problems alone

- Applying no tools or the wrong tools

- Trying a quick fix

- Applying the wrong fix

- Giving feedback in unclear language

- Assuming one problem/one solution

- Failing to educate clients

Some of these issues are more applicable for those auditors who may become consultants, recommending and enacting different organizational fixes, but some of these errors should be addressed by the auditor as a means of ensuring an effective and efficient product. I will address several of Tobey's (2005) issues above in more detail as well as some from a different perspective.

AUDITOR BIAS CHECK

The auditor, in most cases, is not a stakeholder. In some instances, such as when an auditor is internal, they may benefit directly or indirectly from audit results, but usually the auditor remains a somewhat impartial or neutral observer and evaluator. This impartiality allows for a perspective that can be unclouded. However, there may be times when the auditor has misjudged an underlying bias or prejudice toward the organization or even toward the audit as a whole. In these instances, a bias check is needed to ensure that the evaluation has been conducted in an ethical and unbiased manner.

DOUBLE-CHECK RESULTS

There may be times when results are incorrect. Before presenting any data, especially data that may not be well received, a more thorough evaluation may be appropriate. If possible, a second set of eyes may be helpful to determine if there was insufficient data collection or incorrect analyses. While the auditor may assume that their perspective is sufficient, going back and ensuring that all measures were necessary and that data collection was sufficient is helpful. Additionally, there may be some analyses that were entered incorrectly and need revision before presentation to the stakeholders.

COLLECTION MEASURES MISSED

In some audits, a circumstance may arrive where you finish and realize that the tools you used to collect the data were not appropriate or helpful. In some cases, the tools used (e.g., a job satisfaction survey that reveals minimal answers to holistic problems) completely miss the mark of what you were trying to accomplish in the first place. In this instance, it may be helpful to recommend additional measures, as long as they are unobtrusive at this particular point in time. An honest response where you recommend additional data collection to provide richer results may be a helpful way to handle results that fall flat. There are also situations where you may find something in your results that necessitates additional data collection. Similarly, requesting that additional data be collected can help establish additional insight.

SUGGESTING THE WRONG FIX

This error may be more appropriate for those who serve in consulting roles where the expectation is that the contract comes with specific recommendations. In any case, there is an expectation, not an unrealistic one, that the auditor has a deeper understanding of the data and, as such, can provide organizational insight that is not accessible to all. Recommending a wrong fix, where the organization takes your advice and then finds that the solution either didn't work or made the situation worse, can be challenging to overcome and may harm your word-of-mouth reputation. I try, at the beginning of the process, to share that my insight, even with significant data, is limited. As the auditor I am not involved in every facet of the organization, and especially if I have not offered a deep dive into the organization, exposure is probably limited to what I have collected throughout the audit process. Suggesting a slow launch into various recommendations may also help an organization identify if a suggestion may fall flat.

REPORTING RESULTS IN JARGON

As the auditor, you can purposefully select the language you want to use in your report. This means you can avoid language that is unhelpful and unclear. Reports that use jargon, those specialized words that may not be accessible to all, may end up doing more harm than good. Those who engage in a communication audit are, hopefully, competent communicators. Because of this communication element, it is even more pressing and important to be clear in how we talk about our audits to the audience. This means we need to use language that will lead to change and not confusion. When writing a report, you should use simple words and phrases and holistically clear language. Try to minimize abbreviations or acronyms that need continual definition, and then be consistent with the terms you do use. In some organizations, jargon will be acceptable because the group will have a collective understanding of the jargon-filled language. However, in some cases, especially when a report may be communicated to a board of directors or trustees, this jargon may create an obstacle to understanding for those unfamiliar with the terms you, or even the organization, use. The issue here is less about technical jargon and more about simplicity. Make sure you are establishing a credible and simple cadence to help facilitate understanding. Your report should be cohesive, relevant, direct, concise, and concrete. If you are working with one specific individual throughout the process, you may have them review your report for clarity before submitting to the broader audience.

CONFUSION ABOUT AUDIT PURPOSE

The error surrounding audit purpose probably should have been addressed before getting to the results stage. However, even if you communicated the audit purpose clearly from the beginning, there are some who may still, after the audit has been completed or is nearing completion, be unsure of the main point and purpose. If stakeholders remain confused about the audit, I like to go back to materials created during our initial meetings, specifically revelations surrounding the strategic goals. If stakeholders are unsure about why the audit exists or believe it did not meet their expectations, then they will see the audit as being prone to error.

ASSUMING ONE PROBLEM AND ONE SOLUTION

Finally, the audit may have holistic challenges where the auditor or the stakeholders have assumed there is one problem and therefore one solution. In this case, the audit has become a one-size-fits-all prescriptive, not descriptive, tool. If this is a felt need and there seems to be miscommunication from all parties about what the audit can and should help illuminate and solve, then a reorientation may be helpful. An audit will probably reveal more than one problem, and as a result, organizations may be overwhelmed trying to determine which direction to move first. If this is the case, the auditor can help prioritize which issue should be addressed first. It is important to remember, though, that even one singular issue may not have a specific solution and that solving problems can be a multifaceted operation for an organization. The audit may not reveal one problem and one solution, and making this assumption throughout the process can lead to frustrating interactions as the project comes to a close.

When the audit goes wrong, it is in partially up to the auditor to try to identify where the issue arose. In some instances, clearly communicating with stakeholders from the beginning can help solve issues that may hamper final results, but as these challenges have revealed, there are instances when an audit will have problems or errors that arise toward the end of the process. No matter the case, the auditor must remain steadfast and committed to the ultimate goal of helping the organization solve those pressing communication challenges. The next section will help auditors understand how to communicate results, especially those results that are discouraging for the stakeholder.

Results-Based Challenges

This section probably should be called "How to Share Bad News" because when we have to communicate different obstacles on the way to effective communication, it can end up as a conversation that resounds with bad news.

This section will detail how to share results that are not positive and will dive into specific issues that may be of concern when sharing audit results.

SHARING BAD NEWS

Unfortunately, feedback is often dreaded. It can be extremely hard to deliver and receive bad news, and while we like to think that business is not personal, it really is a transparent, vulnerable process where, in many cases, one's entire identity is wrapped up in a job (Miscenko & Day, 2015). Because of this reality, sharing bad news, especially about an organization and potentially individual employees within the organization, can cause great anxiety and consternation. As the potential messenger of bad news, the auditor is in a precarious situation. As mentioned before in this book, stakeholders may have preconceived notions, and you, the auditor, may be brought in to reinforce these ideas. If your results do not mesh with their ideas, this could lead to difficult conversations. Or if the data you collected reveals substantial holistic problems that need immediate attention, especially personnel decisions, this can lead to incredibly tense interactions. The following ideas may help you consider how to share bad news in a way that is both helpful and effective.

REPORTING INFORMATION DIRECTLY

When writing my audit reports, I try to report only the facts. In other words, my data drives my argument. In this regard, you remove some of the inference and perception from the process. Because of this, there tends to be a firmer understanding that this is not just my read on the situation but rather that my collection methods and analysis revealed these fundamental concerns. When you report your data, report data directly. Present your data in concrete and declarative terms. Avoid perceptions at the beginning, and instead, rely on your process.

FRAME YOUR FINDINGS

Your position or purpose is not to be inherently critical. Instead, you are presenting what you have found through the audit process. Changing your mindset before delivering your report can help you establish clarity about the overall framework. Your goal should be to serve the organization through the completion of this communication audit. Anything that happens as a result of the audit, including hurt feelings, misunderstandings, or disagreements, should be addressed as part of the process, not a personal vendetta. As the auditor, you are collaboratively responsible for the entire process. This is why bringing stakeholders in at the beginning is so important. Once the strategic goals and process are agreed upon, you become the vehicle for information and potentially, but not always, a consultant. Your findings should be presented within the context of the broader organization. Mention where there may be limitations or issues with the data, but frame your findings as helpful conceptualizations of the broader structure of the organization. You are there to help but you are also there to present your findings. Making sure that you revisit the process and share how your results were achieved can also help frame the findings within the audit procedure.

PERSONNEL MATTERS

Often, my audit results reveal substantial personnel issues. There are times when data will clearly identify an issue with organizational structure, especially overloaded administrative positions or mismanaged/misassigned job responsibilities. This is the part of the process that I do not enjoy. When I present my findings, I do not appreciate explicitly mentioning individuals or positions in my report that interview or survey results indicate need to be removed. This can become excruciating, especially if the organization plans on making the report public. Including specific names or positions in a report that will be distributed beyond the stakeholders can damage an already fragile culture. There are times when I will buffer personnel findings with different caveats, especially if there were some differences across responses from organizational members, but I still believe the best matter of course is to skip the euphemisms and present the information clearly and directly. The best-case scenario is that if the report is made public and those who were personally named in the report read the findings, then they may decide to change their behavior or work ethic. However, this cannot be counted on to happen every time.

FOCUS ON THE FUTURE

The delivery of bad news often gets bogged down by present concerns—and for good reason! These are legitimate issues that are impacting the day-to-day operations of the organization. By focusing on the future, though, and not just the present, you give stakeholders an opportunity to creatively solve problems. Again, this is a matter of reframing. Instead of seeing discouraging results in an audit report as catastrophic, see them instead as helpful signposts to greater efficiency and effectiveness. Instead of seeing current challenges as paralyzing, see the report as a roadmap to help guide decision making moving forward. One thing I like to do is send my report before delivering my final presentation. This allows my stakeholders to have a softened blow and to actually digest the information before we begin to discuss or share with the broader organizational audience. Stakeholders who are truly leaders will appreciate the direct approach and the reminder that we need to move forward now that we have access to this information.

Quick Tips

REHEARSE AND PRACTICE (AND EDIT)

At the end of your audit, you will probably either submit a written report to stakeholders or present orally to stakeholders about your findings. We cannot assume that our results will be communicated clearly without first practicing, rehearsing, and editing (if in written form) our final report. Before presenting your report, in whatever format, you should practice delivery of your results in a calculated manner. If there are potentially damaging or disturbing results, you should determine the exact language you want to use to present these findings. Practice your vocal tone and inflection, making sure to sound both empathetic and somewhat unemotional. Remember, you are presenting the facts. This preparation is crucial.

PROVIDE OPPORTUNITIES FOR FEEDBACK

When you provide opportunities for questions, especially for those challenging results, it is important to control that environment. This does not mean you are commanding or disregarding, but it means that you strategically allow for true feedback, not necessarily debate. When you present your findings, you are doing just that: allowing the data you discovered to speak for itself. There may be debate with the methods, but the results should not bring about any contested discussion. Control the conversation by keeping everyone on task and connected to the discussion at hand. It is okay to allow for venting, but keep it focused.

There will be times when you must present unflattering results to your stakeholders. This is part of the audit process. As important as those findings are, the communication of those results is almost equally important. Speak with authority and empathy, be confident in your process, and allow for discussion where appropriate.

ACTIVITIES AND DISCUSSION QUESTIONS

1. Use the space below to forecast any potential audit challenges and, more importantly, how to solve these potential issues.

    _____

    _____

    _____

    _____

    _____

    _____

2. What messaging framework can you use to most effectively communicate your findings?

    _____

    _____

    _____

    _____

_____

_____

3. Perform a quick bias check. Is there anything impeding your judgment as you complete the communication audit?

_____

_____

_____

_____

_____

_____

WHAT WOULD YOU DO?

This chapter offered several different reasons why an audit may go wrong. These reasons include auditor bias, incorrect results, inadequate data collection, ineffective suggestions/fixes, results reported using jargon, confusion about the audit process from the beginning, and you (or your stakeholders) have assumed one problem and subsequently one solution. Consider these different challenges and select one. Then discuss below how you would work to solve the problem, or enter different strategies you could use to overcome one of these issues.

_____

_____

_____

_____

_____

_____

_____

_____

_____

_____

_____

_____

CHAPTER 11

Internal Communication Strategy

T his chapter will help you map out a new communication process based on the results of you communication audit. You will be given different categories for designing an effective communication process.

Communication Process

Communication audits can help organizations prepare for next-level efficiency. However, to encourage effective communication organization-wide, an effective communication process is needed. Figure 11.1 is an "old school" communication process model.

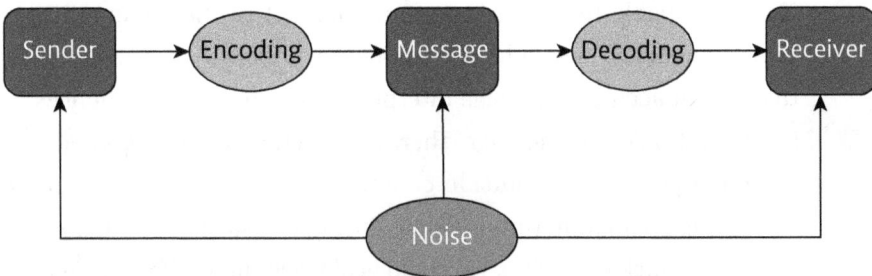

Figure 11.1 Communication Process Model
Copyright © by Freedom Learning Group (CC BY 4.0) at https://courses.lumenlearning.com/wm-organizationalbehavior/chapter/the-process-of-communication/.

There are a few different pillars to consider: sender, message, receiver, and noise.

- **Sender:** In any communication process, the sender is the initial or preliminary communicator. The sender is primarily responsible for initiating the message. Before sending the message, the sender will encode the message, meaning they will translate the information into a digestible message and then literally send the message through symbols that represent ideas or concepts. The sender is the message initiator. They decide what is message-worthy and how to convey the information.

- **Message:** The message is the information conveyed by the sender via words, signs, or symbols. Very literally, the message is the content of the communication process. The message is sent, obviously, by the sender. In many ways the message actually connects the sender and the receiver.

- **Receiver:** In the communication process the receiver is the person who gets the message and tries to decode the information from the sender. Decoding is the process of understanding, trying to decipher or understand what the sender wants to convey through the communication process. The receiver's role is that of interpreter. They are responsible for trying to determine the meaning of the message and understand the sender's true intent.

- **Noise:** Probably the most important element of the communication process model is noise, which in this context refers to anything that distracts from accurate message interpretation. Noise also influences the interpretation of the message. There are several different types of noise, including physical (an outside communication effort by someone or something), semantic (interference during message construction, like jargon or a lack of clarity), psychological (including different elements like biases or prejudices), and physiological (biological or physical impairments that may lead to message confusion). A fifth noise type, cultural noise, has become more popular recently as well.

Unfortunately, we face an increasingly distracting environment. Interestingly, digital marketing experts report that we see an average of around 4,000–10,000 advertisement messages a day (Simpson, 2017). Consider this in the context of other messaging realities. A 2020 study revealed that 350,000 tweets are sent every minute (Sayce, 2020). Instagram users spend around 30 minutes a day on the platform (Newberry, 2021). And approximately 304 billion emails are sent each day (Lynkova, 2021). These numbers are staggering. We are bombarded with information every second of every day. The question for your organization is how can you be distinct? How can your messaging uniquely reach your internal audience? The following steps will help you consider how to use your audit results to inform your internal communication strategy but, even more so, help you develop an internal communication plan.

STEP 1:
THE END GOAL

The first step in determining an internal communication plan is to consider your end goal. What is the vision for your internal strategy? What are you trying to accomplish? A solid communication strategy begins with the knowledge of what you are trying to achieve with your internal communication. Before developing the plan, you should create a vision statement that evokes your communication goal. A well-written vision statement should be short, simple, concise, and clear. A vision statement should position the internal communication strategy as something important and nonnegotiable. An example vision statement could be something like:

> The internal communication strategy at XYZ Organization allows stakeholders to have a common understanding of the organization's communication efforts and will lead to increased employee engagement, a more positive organizational culture, and greater effectiveness and efficiency.

An individual team at an organization may also adopt a communication strategy and could create something more tangible, such as:

> The Human Resource Department at XYZ Organization will deliver prompt and understandable messaging related to

matters of great importance to personnel. We will advocate for our people by creating awareness of our organization's benefits while using our communications to enhance our company culture.

These two vision statements are reminders of the importance of establishing a common footing and a unified message for communication success.

STEP 2:
EVIDENCE-BASED RATIONALE

As discussed throughout this book, evidence-based practices are necessary for communication success. As such, a communication audit should be conducted before, during, and after you create your internal communication strategy. With that said, other evidence can be helpful as you develop communication process management strategies. When building an internal communication strategy, you can consider how you are collecting data related to culture, satisfaction, and effectiveness.

Your cultural dynamics should be approached as a holistic endeavor. Do your communication efforts help people feel connected, or do they make people feel disjointed and confused? Or does your internal communication plan strive for an accessible and equitable strategy that reaches all employees no matter their position, capabilities, or demographic? Collecting cultural data can help you determine the overall connectedness of your communication strategy.

Satisfaction is closely tied to culture. Your internal communication plan should reach employees and help them feel more satisfied in their current position. Recognize that effective internal communication will not solve every problem. It is by no means a panacea. However, effective internal communication can help people feel less frustrated and more satisfied in their jobs. You should collect data that explores the correlation between job satisfaction and your internal communication efforts.

Finally, an internal communication strategy should be effective, and data must be collected that measures this effectiveness. An audit will help you measure the true effectiveness of your communication efforts. We cannot assume that adding a new tool or channel will naturally increase effectiveness; instead, the opposite may be true. No matter how we approach communication efforts, we need to move beyond making decisions that are not based on evidence or driven by driven and instead establish a rationale for communication strategies.

STEP 3:
SYNERGY AND ALIGNMENT

Your internal communication efforts should be aligned with other organizational initiatives. The communication strategy is not a siloed effort and instead drives many, if not all, other organizational decisions; at the very least, it influences how other organizational initiatives are achieved. Your internal strategy should be taken as seriously as other strategic goals of the organization. As your organization discusses other strategic goals, include a conversation about your internal strategy.

STEP 4:
STRATEGY

After determining your communication end goal, collecting and analyzing data to inform decisions, and then assessing other initiatives to determine synergistic alignment, your last step is to actually strategize and create an internal communication plan that is attainable and implementable. Your strategies should connect to your people and may change depending on the scope and efforts of your organization. Your strategies may also change depending on different organizational needs or tools that are available on the market. The most important idea here is to be aware and flexible. Actually establish a coherent plan, be aware of how your plan has been implemented and is received, and then be flexible and ready to adapt and change depending on the needs of your organization and different tools available to achieve your goals. The next section will explore strategy in greater depth.

Internal Communication Strategy

This section emphasizes different strategies for establishing an effective internal communication plan. There are other volumes that explore in greater depth and detail the actual process of creating an internal strategy. However, this section will, at the very least, give you different categories and questions to help you create a tangible and effective formula for reaching internal audiences and stakeholders.

SETTING OBJECTIVES

Similar to the audit process, an internal communication strategy should begin with objectives. As you consider your communication efforts, you should focus on what objectives you want to achieve. Below are a few questions that will help you think strategically about your communication efforts and, more importantly, your strategic objectives.

Questions to Consider

1. What should your internal communication achieve?

2. What do you want people to know, think, or do as a result of your messaging?

3. What channels or platforms are currently used that can help the organization achieve its communication goals?

4. What channels or platforms does the organization currently use that create confusion or are redundant?

5. What feedback have you received that shows any potential obstacles or challenges related to your current strategy?

6. What organizational disconnections do you notice (e.g., cultural, satisfaction, effectiveness, etc.)?

7. Where do the disconnections exist?

8. Are your people prepared to communicate effectively?

9. Do communication-related professional development opportunities exist for members of your organization?

These questions will help you identify potential avenues for exploration. When setting objectives, however, make sure you think in terms of strategic targets. Describe the target you want to achieve and start to diagram the process of how you will achieve this goal. The SMART goals mantra is probably a bit overused, but for our purposes, it can be helpful. You want to make sure your communication objectives are **s**pecific, **m**easurable, **a**chievable, **r**ealistic, and **t**imely. If your objectives hit these different components, you can begin the process of gathering data related to your communication efforts and thus be ready to adapt, evolve, and potentially change depending on your circumstances.

MESSAGING

The buzzword "messaging" is often reserved for external communications: "Your message should resonate with clients and consumers," "You want to make sure your message is on brand," or "Your message should be distinguishable in the marketplace." Much has been written about external messages, but I believe internal messaging is just as important. A clear and consistent internal message will help your organization remain stronger or get even stronger. I really like how StaffBase articulates their internal communication strategy. They focus on three distinct elements: framing, narrative, and message (Jaff, 2015).

- **Framing:** includes an audience analysis of sorts. You want to know what your audience thinks about or understands about a certain topic. In some ways, an audit process can be replicated to determine the audience's perspective about even more specific concepts at the organizational level.

- **Narrative:** the story you tell through your messaging. A narrative arc within the messaging process goes through a journey from a challenge to a destination. There is ultimately a price or a climax as well that must occur for the challenge to be completed. As you think about narrative messaging in your organization, consider where you are, where you want to be, and how you get there through this story-filled lens.

- **Message:** the actual delivered content. In this step, you should think about the end result(s). What is it that should be different about your audience once they read or receive the message? Do you want them to do something different, act in a different way, or think or feel differently than they currently do?

Your messaging should be consistent across the organization; clear, unique or distinguishable; and should lead to some sort of action step.

CHANNEL SELECTION

The means by which you deliver your message is the channel. Channels are, very simply, mediums you can use to send your message out to your preferred audience. Again, we often think about this more externally than internally. Externally, organizations are often cognizant of not overwhelming stakeholders and selecting channels very purposefully. An organization may have a spectacular digital or online presence where they reach hundreds or thousands (or more) people per day, yet when you look at their internal messaging, it may be disjointed or confusing.

When I think of internal communication channels, I almost always think first about different tools. Email can be not only a channel but also a specific communication tool. The difference is not important now, but it is important to note that as you think about channels when developing your internal communication tools, you need to consider what is currently available and accessible and what can be removed as well as added. This is part of the reason why an audit or assessment is so important: An audit allows you to navigate current channels and see their good and bad points.

I want to try to avoid writing about different tools. At the time of this writing, Slack is a popular internal communication platform that utilizes instant messaging, voice and video calls, and different channels or group meeting places for different projects. In some ways it is a project management tool as well as a communication platform. However, years from now Slack may be nonexistent, so offering a detailed review or pro/con list about Slack may not be helpful. Instead, I want to provide a few questions you should consider as you analyze communication channels in your organization.

Questions to Consider

1. What internal channels is my organization currently using?

2. What are the pros and cons of each internal channel?

3. What feedback have you received from your internal stakeholders about each channel?

4. Are there some channels that may be redundant in scope or capability?

5. Are there some channels that may be more accessible for our internal stakeholders?

6. Are we using each channel appropriately?

FREQUENCY

Once you have identified different messages and appropriate channels, you need to determine message frequency. How often do certain messages need to be sent? Do you have messages that lend themselves more to daily, weekly, or even monthly communication? I believe the best advice to offer here is to strive for purposeful repetition. Most internal communication strategies fail because they are not approached with intentionality. Externally, your stakeholders may have to hear/read/consume a message anywhere from 5–20 times for the message to stick, and even then desired results may not be achieved. Instead, internally, consider what your people need to know and how often. Are there more pressing challenges that require additional distribution? Are there timely challenges (e.g., an accounting firm close to tax day) that need to be addressed at specific times during the fiscal year or quarter? These questions matter and should not be taken lightly.

One of the main concerns here is that we send information too frequently or too infrequently. While you may not be able to logically think through every message in your organization, you can begin the process of training people to consider what they say, how, and how often. In some ways this is an issue of training and in others an issue of culture. Either way, frequency matters as you build out your internal communication strategy.

COMMUNICATION UP, DOWN, AND ACROSS

Communication strategies should also recognize that there are different levels of stakeholders across the organization. Obviously, communication looks different depending on the audience and the receiver. This means that communication up to a supervisor or down to an employee or even across the organization between coworkers may look different depending on which direction the message is heading. A communication strategy should think strategically about directionality. What precedents are established that can help you distinguish the appropriate distribution of messages?

When communicating down, you should focus on several different elements, specifically communicating with different groups and development teams and establishing effective and efficient meetings. Often, communicating down involves feedback. All employees want clear objectives and assessment. Two types of feedback are generally warranted: positive feedback, which reinforces good work, and corrective feedback, which urges the employee to change their course of action. Communicating down requires different ideas than communicating up or even across the organization.

Communicating up involves several different ideas, but the main theme is making a conscious effort to affect the perceptions, opinions, and decisions of the people around you, especially those above you. To communicate effectively you must understand the motivations of your people and expectations and be willing to adapt accordingly.

A strategy that diagrams communication across the organization will effectively use several different platforms and perspectives. First, a communication strategy across the organization will effectively use the grapevine, those informal communication outlets. Those who communicate to those on the same level as themselves also have to use different interpersonal skills in different capacities and be willing to be available and collaborative.

Ultimately, an internal communication strategy will recognize different directions for communication and how to reach different audiences depending on whether you are communicating up, down, or across. Generally, a communication strategy will purposefully identify how messages are communicated depending on which direction they are heading within the organization.

DIALOGUE

While recognizing different stakeholders and the necessity to adjust messaging depending on the direction it flows, an effective communication strategy will also emphasize dialogue across the organization and through different departments. Dialogue is important within an organization for several reasons, but for purposes here, a communication strategy should both:

- incorporate dialogue and feedback from stakeholders in an ever-evolving desire to adjust the internal communication process and

- set up means by which dialogue can be incorporated across the organizational structure.

First, it is important to consider feedback loops and a dialogic process when developing or revising an internal communication strategy. Establishing assessment mechanisms, like surveys, that determine stakeholder perceptions should be a part of the process throughout all stages. The audit helps propel this dialogue, but it shouldn't end once the audit process is finalized.

Second, a communication strategy should allow for relationship building across the organization. Mechanisms and structures for dialogue should be developed in and through the communication strategy to allow stakeholders the opportunity to interact. Whether your organization is fully virtual/remote, fully face to face, or a hybrid combination, an effective strategy recognizes that people should build strong professional relationships and subsequently provide spaces for these relationships to develop.

ETHICS

Last but certainly not least, a communication strategy should be ethical. There are several ways to look at ethical communication, but communication across the organization should be civil, respectful, truthful, accessible, and appropriately transparent. If your dialogic feedback indicates an unethical organization ethos, then there needs to be a drastic and dramatic readjustment. People should feel psychologically safe when they provide insight and, by the same token, should recognize that communication with them from their peers or supervisors will be respectful and considerate.

A holistic communication strategy is necessary for organizational success in the 21st century. It is not enough to assume that effective communication will naturally occur. Communication happens all the time, but good, clear, and effective communication is rare. An internal communication strategy is a blueprint that helps organizations achieve successful communication goals. Instead of ignoring a strategy, approach it head on and strive to develop a continuous and holistic approach that identifies mission and vision, key responsibilities and processes, and other functional messages.

A few final thoughts:

- Similar to an audit, as you build your communication plan, identify key performance indicators or metrics that are measurable.

- You can do this by monitoring interaction, incorporating surveys and focus groups, or establishing other analytics.

- Create clear, informative, and engaging messages, and send these messages to the appropriate audience through the appropriate channels.

- Schedule your messages for greatest impact.

- Ask for feedback from key stakeholders.

ACTIVITIES AND DISCUSSION QUESTIONS

Use the template below to craft a preliminary internal communication strategy.

Objectives

Objective 1:

_____

_____

_____

_____

_____

Objective 2:

_____

_____

_____

_____

_____

Objective 3:

_____

_____

_____

_____

Message

Messaging Framework:

_____

_____

_____

_____

Channel Selection:

_____

_____

_____

_____

Channel Selection:

_____

_____

_____

_____

WHAT WOULD YOU DO?

After completing your audit, you realize that the organization you are working with has several holistic communication issues. The stakeholders you are working with realize this but want you to fix the issue in an unethical manner. Specifically, they want you to work in a plan where you monitor different internal messages without employees knowing (something akin to an email monitoring system). How would you handle this situation? What would you say to those stakeholders?

_____

_____

_____

_____

_____

_____

_____

_____

_____

_____

_____

CHAPTER 12

Infusing an Audit Into Organizational Culture

T his chapter will help you create organizational change based on the findings of your audit and their suggestions for new communication processes.

Organizational Culture

The study of organizational culture has become more complex. I believe the challenges occur in part because we struggle to identify what culture really entails. Deal and Kennedy (1982) believe *organizational culture* is defined as a set of values, beliefs, assumptions, and symbols that define the way an organization functions. In reality, though, organizational culture is more readily defined as "how we do things around here." This means a conversation about organizational culture is really about organizational rules and norms that are either established through actual policies and procedures or developed through informal means.

Many different organizational components are linked to organizational culture, including competitive advantage (Barney, 1986), leadership (Schein, 2010), unethical behavior (Umphress et al., 2010), recruitment (Braddy et al., 2006), and retention (Sheridan, 1992). Culture, in addition, can help us understand how organizations solve problems and resolve different issues or challenges. Some of these challenges can be revealed through communication audits.

There are distinguishing factors of organizational culture that are helpful for a conversation about infusing audit results into an organization. Sanchez (2011) identifies four elements of organizational culture: strategy, structure, people, and processes. It is helpful to think about audit infusion from all four of these elements and discuss how results can be implemented to enhance strategy, improve structure, build relationships, and enhance processes.

STRATEGY

Communication audits can be positioned across the organization as a strategy framework. The fundamental purpose of an audit is not to build a strategy: The process is more prescriptive, but thankfully, an audit can serve as a bridge to a strategic plan. Unfortunately, most organizational efforts fail because of a lack of strategy. The audit, then, provides a basis and a framework for why change is needed and establishes a starting point for a conversation about strategic implementation.

From a strategic perspective, an internal communication audit should remind decision makers that they must be aligned in their strategic thinking. Endorsing, from the beginning, a process that leads to strategic implementation will position the audit as a legitimate expenditure of time and effort. The audit can give decision makers data that they can rely on to provide governance and oversight and will, hopefully, reinforce their assumptions.

Unlike audits that only provide data, strategic communication audits give the organization a direction and a process to follow to achieve maximum effectiveness. Individuals will struggle with the audit process if they do not see a strategic end goal. While it is true that every organization has their own way of developing and implementing strategies, an audit, at the very least, can establish a common language and a needs-based approach.

Strategy implementation, the process of turning ideas or plans into action, is particularly necessary for communication goals. Organizational success, from a communication standpoint, rests on the organization's ability to implement manageable goals and execute strategic initiatives effectively. If planned appropriately, an audit can even be used simultaneously to assess the effectiveness of communication within the organization as it relates to a strategic plan. The audit process can even be applied to strategic initiatives.

Generally, when positioning a communication audit as a legitimate and valuable expense, make sure to communicate to those in charge that the audit is the first step in designing and enhancing organizational strategy. Positioning the audit as an isolated or siloed event will not create a sense of return on investment that is needed to achieve actual change across the organization. Instead, the audit should be an important part of organizational culture at large and, in essence, should be established early on as just one step in the larger strategic process the organization has identified. When I conduct audits, I always like to position the audit experience as a necessary data-gathering event that then informs strategic decisions. You must be prepared to explain how this audit fits within the broader organizational strategic structure.

As a strategic complement, the audit will give you and your client a framework for success. Approaching the audit as a necessary part of strategic alignment and implementation will, hopefully, put an onus on the audit as something that cannot be ignored and can be applied across the organization at large.

STRUCTURE

One argument for audit implementation is the potential for improved organizational structure. An organization's structure includes the workflow and communication flow that is embedded within an organization. Structure can include reporting issues, like who a supervisee answers to during a project, or how the hierarchy, or lack thereof, of an organization manifests itself. Ultimately, a communication audit can reveal structural issues, especially those related to how communication flow is achieved in relation to communicating up, down, and across the organization.

As you consider an organization's culture and the positive role an audit can play in that cultural development, you may want to consider encouraging an audit to encourage effective communication up the chain of command. For instance, an audit may reveal that employees do not feel safe or encouraged to share their thoughts or opinions to their supervisor, and more practically, an audit can direct consults or auditors to determine new approaches to encourage supervisors to share information with their supervisors. In addition, an audit can reveal issues or challenges with reporting or communicating down in instances when a supervisor or manager communicates with supervisees.

An audit can easily reveal inconsistencies, questionable methods, or inefficiencies. Finally, an audit can reveal challenges when organizations strive to communicate across the organization. In other words, when peer-to-peer or coworker-to-coworker communication has been analyzed, an audit can reveal when and where breakdowns occur when teammates need to complete projects. In this way, an audit can be helpful for analyzing communication across the organization.

As a cultural tool, an audit that reveals inefficient structural processes or programs can provide a useful and valuable perspective. Instead of relying on instinct or "feel," an audit provides data-driven realities that show where structures do not work or are not as effective. In this vein, an audit can be a helpful holistic tool for communication at the institutional or organizational level.

A periphery benefit of audits is the potential to identify structural personnel inefficiencies. While the audit's primary purpose is not personnel-based, an added benefit of this type of analysis is the potential for the audit to reveal redundancies in job roles and responsibilities. In this way, an audit can provide data for transforming the hierarchy of an organization and may provide stakeholders with information regarding new positions that may be necessary.

As a cultural categorization, an organization's structure should "work" for the organization. There is not a one-size-fits-all approach to how organizations design their personnel structure or even their holistic communication strategy. Yet an audit will help individual organizations, and even departments within an organization, find out what works more effectively for their people. In this regard, an audit can be a useful tool for improving an organization's structure and subsequently improving an organization's culture. A communication audit can provide revelatory information about the organization's workflow and messaging.

PEOPLE

As an organizational culture tool, audits can show supervisors where relationships need additional support. Communication is integral across the organization, and I am guilty, like some others are, of focusing more on output, process, procedure, and operations and forgoing the appropriate perspective when it comes to relationships. The traditional workplace involves many different factors, including people, processes, and plans. People need to feel connected to their organization, and this is achieved in part through relationships. When the socialization and assimilation processes have been achieved to maximum effectiveness, people tend to feel more connected to their organization (Strawser et al., 2021). The reality is that clear communication and thorough relationship building can help encourage and sustain an employee's sense of belonging. Employees must feel connected to the organization.

An audit can help reveal instances where relationships may be broken or not as effective as they could be. In this regard, an audit can really help provide insight into relational disharmony and potential conflict. Employees must feel heard. If they are routinely frustrated with their role within the organization and if they perceive they have a disharmonious existence with their coworkers, the culture at large will struggle and individual employees will not be as effective.

Audits can help organizations understand how communication has, is, and will impact relationships. For example, an audit can reveal levels of dissatisfaction or satisfaction with the job itself, different manifestations of positive/supportive or negative/dissenting messaging, as well as different levels of connection and identification employees feel across their organization. The audit is primarily a tool to measure effectiveness but it can reveal interesting relational elements as well.

From a culture perspective, then, it behooves organizations to use audits to assess relationships across the institution. Instead of relying on a gut feeling, organizations can use audits to gather data-driven insights that can then encourage new directions for building and sustaining relationships. Especially today, as remote work continues to increase (Hickman & Pendall, 2018), healthy employee relationships can be a premium distinction for organizations in the recruitment, hiring, and retention process.

Using audits to build and improve relationships across the organization can be a daunting task. The auditor must be careful to not add negative presuppositions into the audit questionnaire. This is especially difficult for internal auditors/consultants who may be privy to relational information, leading them to assume that one individual or a series of individuals are the primary problem. Allow the audit to speak for you, and collect data that shows that these relational issues exist and where they are most prevalent or pressing. The audit, through all of the data collection measures already identified, can provide a well-rounded relational perspective that goes beyond he/she/they said and instead provides robust information surrounding holistic relational issues. In this way, an audit can become a central driving factor for organizational culture and moving an organization toward sustainable positive relationships.

PROCESSES

Audits can encourage more effective strategy, improve structure, help organizations consider how to build relationships and enhance processes. Businesses must continually strive for maximum efficiency. Process improvement involves identifying, analyzing or assessing, and ultimately improving existing processes within an organization. Organizations are living, breathing organisms or evolving works in progress that never fully arrive at maximum effectiveness. The most impactful and most efficient organizations, though, strive for consistent analysis of operations and processes. As such, the ability of organizations to maximize their processes and even approach their overall structure from a process perspective allows for analysis to focus on how the organization can continue to improve (Reay et al., 2019).

If we want to transform organizations, we have to do so one process at a time. Communication audits allow organizations to identify potential errors or issues with current communication processes and work toward improving those barriers that create inefficiencies. As a valuable contributor to organizational culture, audits can provide procedural breakdowns, and by surveying people within the organization, an audit can suggest new and improved mechanisms for change.

Employees today put a premium on communication systems, channels, and frequency. It is amazing how much time managers and supervisors spend in meetings or communicating expectations. In addition, the sheer breadth of work activities that hinge on effective communication is immense. Communication is an ever-changing process in organizations, and as new individuals are brought in, and culture shifts, communication changes and either defines the environment or adapts to the organizational culture and climate.

For decades, organizations were presented with a communication process model that looks something like this the one in Figure 12.1 (this process model is a little more advanced than the one in Chapter 11):

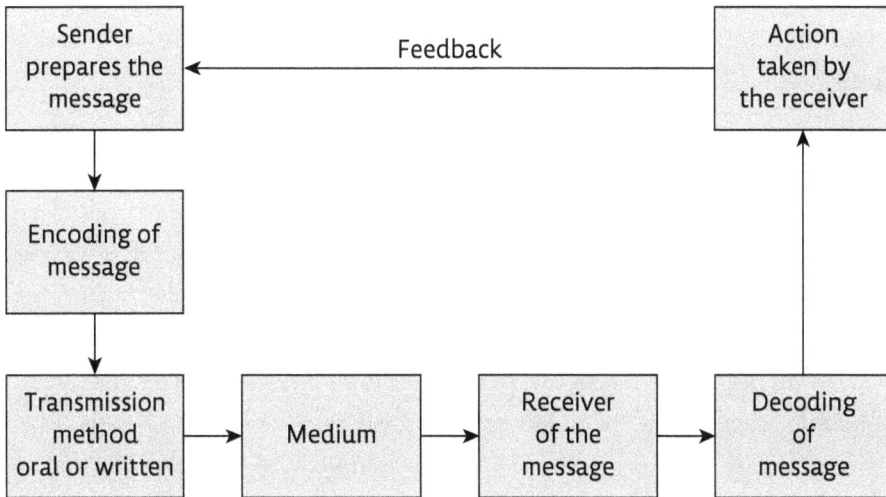

Figure 12.1 Communication Process Steps
"Communication Process Steps," https://lnct.ac.in/wp-content/uploads/2020/04/UNIT-3-NOTES-Communication-skills-English-for-Communication-BT103.pdf. Copyright © by LNCT Group.

As I've said before, the basic fundamental principles of this model are still relevant. There are still senders (those who, very literally, send the message); messages are still encoded (putting the message into a specialized format); messages are still transmitted (through oral, written, or nonverbal means); there is still a medium (a channel that transmits the message); a receiver still hears, sees, or reads the message; the message is still decoded (analyzed and interpreted by the receiver); and then an action is taken (and even an inaction is an action), thus ending with feedback provided back to the sender in some capacity. These fundamental communication realities probably will never change. Yet the information transferred, number of messages, channels available for transmittance, and overall distractions senders and receivers experience everyday have created unprecedented communication confusion. The communication audit, then, allows for communication processes to be made visible and hopefully succinct. An audit that addresses these fundamental procedural categories while exploring where communication breakdown occurs, and how it occurs, can aid overall organizational efficiency. Auditors, then, from a culture standpoint, would do well to utilize audits as a tool to explore broader communication implications across organizations, assessing methods, models, frequencies, and overall effectiveness of message transference.

NAVIGATING PERFORMANCE

The elements mentioned above provide a structure to consider how audits can impact organizational efficiency. However, it is important to note that without people, organizations would cease to function. People can be evaluated through audits by focusing on human performance improvement.

Human performance improvement (HPI) is a comprehensive approach to consulting that focuses on "organizational goals, a systemic approach based on desired results, a focus on performance accomplishments and performance, linkage of performance analysis to the job, analysis of performance gaps, and identification of interventions that will close the performance gaps" (Tobey, 2005, p. 154). It is my guess that most of your clients, both internal and external, want to improve employee performance. To improve HPI, Tobey (2005) identifies three different intervention types:

> **Motivation interventions:** Through this intervention, incentives (like rewards) are infused into the organization, the hope being that performance will increase because of this new motivation.

> **Structure/process interventions:** A structural intervention highlights different changes in organizational structure, like operations, work processes, and even relationships, to hopefully influence performance.

> **Knowledge/skill interventions:** This intervention is fundamentally training, as new knowledge and skills are transferred to employees in ways that will lead to improved performance and results.

Audits can be extremely helpful for evaluating bigger picture organizational or cultural issues that directly impact human performance. Like communication audits, HPI begins by identifying organizational results and performance (Tobey, 2005). HPI is similarly big picture, as it establishes recommendations for issues that may have solutions that go beyond training. An audit can pinpoint organizational personnel pain points, especially those related to human performance, if the appropriate data collection methods are utilized.

Cultural Infusion

Audits are only successful if all stakeholders see value in the audit's data and completion. With that said, the organization must do more to enact true organizational change. It is not enough to just bring in someone to audit an organization; instead, there should be an environment of accountability related to how the organization uses the data. Specifically, organizations should foster a culture of continuous improvement. While certainly ironic, the audit does not end when the report is completed. Instead, stakeholders should practice continuous observation of different categorizations identified by the auditor. Constant observation, then, related to the organization's communication is necessary for cultural infusion. If organizational culture is really about organizational rules and norms that are either established through actual policies and procedures or that are developed through informal means, then an audit can, and should, function as a means of continuous evaluation.

Communication audits and, by association, auditors can become culture drivers, not just culture observers. While an audit is primarily evaluative, it can be a forward-looking tool that helps organizations consider their goals, rules, and norms in relation to the broader organizational structure as well as in relation to relationships across the organization. Organizations should never cease to keep improving. Continually monitoring communication across the organization, as well as relationships throughout, will help establish a culture and climate of growth and effectiveness. Keep track of audit findings and consider making a communication audit a yearly endeavor. Make sure to specify problematic issues as well as opportunities for growth and then use those determinations to conduct appropriate audits in the future.

ACTIVITIES AND DISCUSSION QUESTIONS

How may your audit results influence the following culture elements?

Strategy:

_____

_____

_____

_____

_____

Structure:

_____

_____

_____

_____

_____

People:

_____

_____

_____

_____

_____

Processes:

_____

_____

_____

_____

_____

WHAT WOULD YOU DO?

There are many different cultural elements in organizations that can threaten efficiency. Imagine you are an employee who notices several cultural issues or challenges and wants to avoid discussing specifics with a supervisor. How would you suggest a communication audit as a vehicle to address cultural issues?

_____

_____

_____

_____

_____

_____

_____

_____

_____

CHAPTER 13

Using Results to Inform Organizational Training

T his chapter will help you use your results to think through designing organizational training initiatives. You will be given umbrella communication training topics and will receive a crash course in training and development for communication-based topics.

Sadly, some organizations tend to view training and development as a necessary evil. In my experience, I have been brought into an organization on many occasions to "check a training box," meaning employees, leaders, or customers indicated a need and the quick fix was a recommended half-day or full-day training initiative. I have found these attempts to be excruciatingly unhelpful for all parties. Despite these issues, I am a firm believer in corporate training when it is centered on meeting evidence-based needs.

Organizational Training

I'm sure most individuals have a love-hate relationship with organizational training. Even more so, I'm sure some "love to hate" training. But when approached from an evidence-based perspective, corporate training can be extremely helpful. Organizational training is generally provided by the organization to employees for the purpose of enhancing job performance. Training initiatives are developed with the perspective of professional development. Training, done well, will genuinely help employees be more effective, may increase job efficiency, and could enhance company culture.

While professional development has always been important, we are seeing an influx of younger employees who care deeply about professional development opportunities (Strawser et al., 2021).

Organizational training takes many forms, but there is a progression or a process. Typically, training starts when employees are onboarding. Onboarding includes the initial conversation with new employees where they given instruction on policies, procedures, and general daily operations. A good onboarding program should set employees up for future success in training initiatives. Once onboarding is complete, training ensues. Training focuses specifically, in most cases, on skill development. This is why, from a communication perspective, training can be helpful, although some believe development should be more focused on soft skills. While training topics can be multifaceted, communication corporate training and development can help enhance communication skills.

In *Training and Development: Communicating for Success*, Beebe et al. (2013) define *training* as "the process of developing skills in order to perform a specific job or task more effectively" (p. 5). The goal of training, then, is greater performance. From a communication skill perspective, training can focus on listening, speaking/presenting, leading, managing, providing feedback, and relating. These skills can be refined and summarized as presentation skills, team skills, and interpersonal skills (Beebe et al., 2013).

Communication Topics in Organizational Training

PRESENTATION SKILLS

Presentation skills are fundamental to organizational success. Unfortunately, this is often the forgotten communication skill in corporate training. While somewhat significant focus is applied to public speaking and presentation skills during high school and college, organizations tend to forget the importance of continued training in this area. The expectation is that employees come to the organization already well prepared in this area, and that is not necessarily the case. Presentation skills have an impact on how we are perceived not just within the organization but outside of it as well.

When delivering training that focuses on presentation skills, two key areas are important to consider:

- Make sure you encourage your trainees to be audience-centered speakers. Audience-centered speakers know their audience and are prepared to adapt a message to suit the needs and expectations of the audience.

- Reinforce the importance of clear communication. Your trainees should know that their presentations should have a central idea that must be communicated clearly. This focused messaging should be logical, well organized, and supported by evidence.

Presentations should also be delivered in a manner that is engaging. Effective presentations have clear delivery mechanisms that engage the audience and keep them connected to the speaker and the material. A few foundational delivery concepts include:

- Maximizing eye contact

- Expressing emotions with appropriate facial expressions

- Using purposeful gestures

- Speaking loudly and clearly

- Using vocal inflection that appropriately incorporates an effective pace, rate, pitch, and volume

- Using presentation aids (e.g., graphs, slides, etc.) that enhance the message and do not distract from it

These helpful delivery reminders can be useful even for those who have had presentation training before. There are resources that can help you develop appropriate presentation skills training. These are two of my favorites:

Atwood, C. G. (2017). *Presentation skills training.* ATD Workshop Series.
Beebe, S. A., & Mottet, T. P. (2016). *Business and professional communication: Principles and skills for leadership.* (3rd ed.) Pearson.

TEAM SKILLS

Teamwork has become an incredibly popular buzzword. Just recently I was asked to facilitate a session on "high-impact teams." This focus on teamwork is great for communication experts because all aspects of teamwork include some communicative element. Unlike groups, which include a collection of individuals, a team works toward a specific goal or purpose. Training that is focused on teamwork can be bigger picture and focus on organizational culture as a whole or teamwork generally.

From a communication standpoint, teamwork training can focus on a variety of topics. Trust will always be crucial to successful team deliverables. However, there are several that tend to emphasize team performance. Teamwork training can be utilized to help teams define their mission, strategic goals, and plan of action and can help establish a baseline understanding for communication within the team. As such, cooperation can be discussed as a team-focused element. Teams should also have training that addresses solving problems and forward-thinking strategies. I also like to include elements for assessing team performance as part of my teamwork training. Finally, teamwork training can also include supporting each other and practical tips to succeed before, during, and after conflict.

The good news is that interactive teamwork training works. If training content is dull and stale, then teamwork training may fall flat, but encouraging training through simulation and experiential learning can encourage team members to take their team membership seriously. Collaborative teams are integral to workplace success and they cannot function without effective communication.

I have included a sample training agenda below for a session on high-impact teams and creative problem solving.

TRAINING AGENDA

Content Summary: *High-Impact Teams and Creative Problem Solving*

Morning: High Impact Teams

Afternoon: Creative Problem Solving

As work-related tasks become more complex, the need and demand for high-impact teams that perform at the highest levels is greater than ever. We know that 21st-century problems need creative solutions.

(continued)

Creative energy is at its best in collaborative teams that are focused on tangible solutions. This session will be helpful, as attendees will evaluate their own leadership style, assess their own team's performance, learn how to utilize power and influence, create and sell creative ideas through convergent and divergent thinking, and understand high-performing teams and threats to teamwork and collaborative creative problem solving.

Deliverables

Participants will:

- Understand the communication process specific to leading others, reasons for communication breakdown, and what constitutes organizational culture.
- Gain proven approaches to develop effective internal messages around organizational and team goals.
- Unlock components of personal leadership and effective teamwork.
- Engage in activities that enhance strategic thinking.

9:00 a.m.	Introductions: self; participants
9:15 a.m.	Participants complete first activity: *Personal Leadership Assessment*
9:30 a.m.	Team foundations: culture; SMART objectives; roles and norms; developing leaders
10:30 a.m.	Leading and managing high-impact teams: assessing team performance; high-impact threats
11:30 a.m.	Participants complete second activity: *Managing the Message*
11:45 a.m.	Break
12:00 p.m.	Working lunch: Diagnosing problems: misalignment, culture, and the client
1:00 p.m.	Solving problems creatively and passionately: convergent and divergent thinking; power, influence, and persuasion
2:00 p.m.	Closing thoughts

There are resources that can help you develop appropriate teamwork skills training. These are two of my favorites:

Katzenbach, J. R., & Smith, D. K. (2015). *The wisdom of teams: Creating the high-performance organization.* Collins Business Essentials.

Lencioni, P. (2002). *The five dysfunctions of a team: A leadership fable.* Jossey-Bass.

INTERPERSONAL SKILLS

The topic of interpersonal skills as a training area is multifaceted and can include several different subcategories. While there are other interpersonal skills to consider in the workplace, listening and managing conflict tend to be integral to workplace relationships. It is first important to know that we cannot and should not deemphasize differences in the workplace. An inclusive workplace is one where various identities are represented. The workplace should not be one homogenous group but instead should function as a living, breathing, working organism in the midst of difference. For this reason, workplace relationships become the lynchpin of organizational success. Differences exist in the workplace, but I like how Beebe and Mottet (2016) focus on social style, cultural, gender, and generational differences as key differentiators in the modern organization. Adapting to these differences will separate functional from dysfunctional organizations. In the midst of these differences, encouraging an environment that emphasizes listening, relationships, and conflict management can help overcome many issues.

Listening to each other can help solve significant relational problems. Hearing is not listening. We listen, or should listen, to understand. As we do this, we have to overcome different obstacles, including distractions and our own biases and preconceived notions. Training employees to listen can be extremely beneficial despite the fact that it is time consuming and difficult. Generally, we want to encourage trainees to listen well by turning off distractions and focusing attention. We can also focus on the appropriate response to different messages. We should respond accordingly but especially respond empathetically.

Listening to each other for the purpose of understanding can help negate conflict early on. No matter how proactive organizations are, conflict still exists. It is important to note that conflict can lead to positive outcomes, such as avoiding groupthink, vetting ideas, and creativity. Conflict at work cannot be ignored. Instead, you can train people how to deal with conflict effectively by encouraging trainees to understand their own conflict style and then establishing ground rules for conflict management. Whenever we want to manage conflict, we should avoid making the conflict personal, monitor the emotions of the room and the individuals involved in the conflict, and focus on the problem and next steps.

I have provided a sample agenda below that reflects a training curriculum focused on emotional intelligence, something central to the interpersonal element.

TRAINING AGENDA

Content Summary: *Emotional Intelligence*

Effective communication skills are essential to being productive and successful in the workplace and in service to the customer. Emotionally intelligent employees are in high demand, and as the importance placed on communication skills continues to rise, the need for training sessions that offer concrete communication skills are crucial. To address this concern, participants who attend this workshop will have targeted communication skills training that focuses on developing 21st-century emotional intelligence.

Deliverables

Participants will:

- Understand the importance and necessity of emotional intelligence for 21st-century employees.
- Discuss and identify skills and behaviors that constitute an effective, or competent, communicator.
- Perform self-assessments that analyze unique skills and opportunities for growth in the realm of emotional intelligence.
- Use emotional intelligence guidelines and best practices to solve workplace communication challenges.

(continued)

9:00 a.m.	Introductions: self; participants
9:15 a.m.	Participants complete first activity: *"Think-Pair-Share": What makes an effective communicator?* *Think through those who you believe are effective communicators? What do they do well?* *Think through those who you consider ineffective communicators? What do they do that makes them ineffective?*
9:30 a.m.	Session overview; agenda
9:35 a.m.	Communication in a connected world: Building and sustaining 21st-century relationships
9:50 a.m.	What is emotional intelligence, and why does it matter?
10:20 a.m.	Fitting in: personality and EQ in the workplace; perceiving and managing emotions
10:50 a.m.	Break
11:00 a.m.	Participants complete second activity: *Interpersonal Skills Self-Assessments (Identifying Strengths and Challenges)*
11:30 a.m.	Human behavior and communication characteristics: making an impact
12:00 p.m.	Working lunch Skills training overview: *Listening; Verbal and Nonverbal Skills* Listening; intentional questions; authenticity; body language
1:00 p.m.	Best practices: Guidelines Part 1 *Paving the Way* (EQ consortium) Best practices: Guidelines Part 2 *Doing the Work of Change* (EQ consortium) Best practices: Guidelines Part 3 *Evaluating Change* (EQ Consortium)
2:00 p.m.	Closing thoughts

The Role of the Communication Trainer

Communication experts can serve the broader corporate world as trainers. Communication trainers, at their core, teach communication skills and design training programs. The communication trainer, then, is not just a communication expert but is also a teacher. This fundamental reality, trainer as teacher, should help provide a philosophical framework for the communication trainer's functionality in organizations.

As with any training, communication-specific training should be focused on the needs of the organization. I have always felt that it is easier for me to be an outside trainer. Those who are in-house trainers have the benefit of understanding organizational culture, but like consulting in general, that outside voice and perspective can be helpful. The communication trainer, though, whether internal or external, has an opportunity to help others become more skilled in a variety of different areas.

The communication trainer has a great opportunity to enact true organizational change through purposeful initiatives. The trainer, though, must also be an effective communicator. Frei and Beebe (2019) argue that a communication trainer should have effective presentation skills (both verbal and nonverbal delivery), relational skills (including listening), and group facilitation skills.

I appreciate the National Communication Association Training and Development Division's list of best practices for communication training. The best practices are listed below, but for those interested, they are expanded on in the following book:

Wallace, J. D., & Becker, D. (2019). *The handbook of communication training: A best practices framework for assessing and developing competence.* Routledge.

Best Practices for Communication Training Competence, Accountability, and Transparency

Best Practice 1: Maintain transparency to clients and trainees.

- Those involved in training and development acknowledge a framework of best practices that provides structure for their training and consulting.

- Trainers and consultants should have readily available standards to which their activities can be evaluated by participants. Language should include demonstrable benchmarks.

- Trainers and consultants must abide by a documented code of ethics that is easily attainable by clients and assessment groups.

Best Practice 2: Use accessible methods.

- Trainers and consultants must have identifiable deliverables that can be internally and externally assessed.

- Trainers should be able to demonstrate expertise in training transfer.

Best Practice 3: Demonstrate technology proficiency.

- Trainers should have proficiency in technology needed for delivering and executing training content.

- Trainers should have proficiency in digital technology.

Best Practice 4: Demonstrate professional development.

- Subject and performance competency should be acquired and maintained.

- Professional development should provide leverage for the communication trainer.

Best Practice 5: Develop and maintain organizational expertise.

- Communication trainers and consultants should be familiar with organizational catalysts for training, such as leadership, management, planning, and culture.

- Communication trainers and consultants should be familiar with employee catalysts for training, such as career development, human resources, innovativeness, selection, and appraisal.

Best Practice 6: Demonstrate effective and appropriate instructional design.

- Communication training should be built around implementable models of instructional design.

- Instructional design should accommodate different learning styles and their corresponding instructional methods.

Best Practice 7: Demonstrate communication proficiency.

- Communication trainers should demonstrate executable communication proficiencies, including but not necessarily limited to presentation skills, interpersonal skills, organizational culture, and group techniques.

These best practices provide a wonderful framework for communication trainers. Generally, communication trainers should be client-centered, competent, subject matter experts, and well versed in instructional methods and educational technology.

Needs-Centered Training Model

The logic here bears repeating. If we want training to be recognized as valuable and to enhance job performance, it should meet actual needs, not just perceived needs, of the organization. For this reason, I love the needs-centered training model (see Figure 13.1) developed by Beebe et al. (2013), which focuses on the following elements/process:

1. **Analyze organizational/training needs:** The entire model hinges on analyzing needs. Without a proper needs assessment (see previous chapters), training will not be valuable or useful.

2. **Analyze the training task:** A task analysis allows you to understand key elements of the training end goal.

3. **Develop training objectives:** Training or learning objectives include those outcomes you want your trainees to achieve.

4. **Organize training content:** Draft the information trainees need to know, and describe skills or behaviors they need to demonstrate.

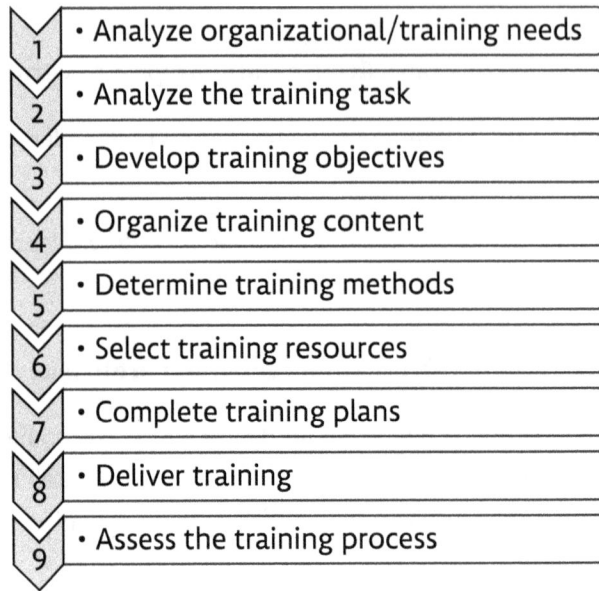

| Figure 13.1 Needs-Centered Training Model

5. **Determine training methods:** Develop effective methods of presenting training information that facilitate your learning objectives.

6. **Select training resources:** Decide what you will have to prepare to present your information.

7. **Complete training plans:** Create a comprehensive training plan.

8. **Deliver training:** Deliver an engaging and interactive training presentation.

9. **Assess the training process:** Evaluate training effectiveness.

Ultimately, your communication training should be audience-centered, and to do that it must be needs-centered. The needs-centered training approach is helpful for recognizing that trainee needs should drive the process throughout the training partnership.

Fundamentally, communication training is skill-based. However, it is also helpful to consider your training goals from the perspective of learning domains. As you consider your training goals, ask yourself, "What do the trainees need to know (cognitive knowledge), think (affect), and do (behavior)?" These learning domains, developed initially by Bloom (1956), have guided training initiatives for decades. As you develop training, you have to consider the end goal: Do you want your trainees to know more communication content, find it more valuable than they do pretraining, or do you want them to successfully complete new skills? These questions will help you move toward a needs-centered approach to training.

Previously in this volume, we discussed needs assessments. The gathering of information through a needs assessment can help you truly develop needs-centered training curriculum. No matter how you collect data (e.g., surveys, interviews, focus groups, or observation), what you collect should inform your training decisions (Beebe, 2019).

Results-Informed Training

The logic of a needs-centered training approach is clear. Without identifiable needs, training will fall short of any intended strategic goal. Instead, it will be a time-wasting effort for the trainer, the trainee(s), and the organization. However, an approach that focuses first on the audience and subsequently the needs of the organization will have lasting and hopefully substantial results.

What does this all mean for us, assessors of communication in organizations? Well, as our process throughout this volume indicates, a communication audit should focus on the stakeholder. And for our purposes, an audit helps us gather information that can help establish a clear results-informed training curriculum. In this way, our audit serves both as a gatekeeper and as evidence. As gatekeeper, the audit presents an initial rationale and a mechanism for assessing organizations and positioning training as a potential solution. As evidence, an audit provides results-informed training suggestions. This should not be taken lightly. Training that is not informed by results will not be effective.

Once the training is conducted, however, our assessment is not over. I love how Deborah Tobey (2005) identifies the data collection step of her training needs assessment process. Tobey believes that we need to collect data before, during, and after the training initiative in order to identify performance, learning, and learner needs. More specifically, we need to understand required performance, learners' current performance, required skills and knowledge, learners' current skills and knowledge, and learners' needs. Our efforts, then, never stop. The cycle continues as we identify organizational needs and provide training to hopefully meet those challenges or opportunities.

Training 101

A chapter on corporate training would not be complete without a reminder that when we design training, we must be audience-centered. This means our training should be interactive, engaging, and well designed.

After we have assessed organizational needs—however that process manifests itself—we need to design the training. When designing training, I like to first look for exemplars in the marketplace. Have others been conducting training on topics like conflict management, and if so, what does their training include? This assumes training is accessible and available for reference. Referencing what others in the market are doing should not limit your own creativity when designing training. Instead, it allows you to know whether or not you are on the right track. Training should also be aligned with organizational goals. At this point, we should hope that our audit has identified needs and that the strategic goals we discussed with the stakeholders before the audit took place remain intact. If so, we can align our training goals with those strategic organizational goals and also with the results of the audit itself. What follows should be a clear identification of the objectives of the training itself.

When developing training objectives, use active verbs, clear and measurable outcomes, and think specifically about what the trainee will receive as a result of the training. Conduct the training in a way that is not focused on the trainer. While it may be easier to stand in front of your audience and lecture, it is not as helpful to attendees. Instead, encourage deep thinking, discussion, reflection, and as much hands-on training as possible. Finally, you want to measure your actual training results. Position the training mechanism as an evaluative process where you assess not just the programmatic effectiveness from the perspective of the trainee but also the organizational effectiveness. In other words, did the training actually accomplish what it was supposed to? If not, reassess and try again. If it did work, reflect on why.

The Goal of Training

I believe training is a means to an end, not the end itself. When we see training as primarily a mechanism to help support employees, keep employees engaged, and increase productivity, then we will (hopefully) refuse mediocre training that is not informed by results. Training should not be a check-the-box data dump. Instead, it should be needs-centered, results-informed, and purposeful.

ACTIVITIES AND DISCUSSION QUESTIONS

1. Which training topics have been revealed as areas of urgent need based on the results of your audit?

    _____

    _____

    _____

    _____

    _____

    _____

2. What training format may be most helpful for your organization?

    _____

    _____

    _____

    _____

    _____

    _____

3. Which communication training best practice resonates most with you, and why?

_____

_____

_____

_____

_____

_____

4. If you could articulate one goal for training, what would it be?

_____

_____

_____

_____

_____

_____

WHAT WOULD YOU DO?

Your communication audit reveals an issue with organizational conflict. You have presented your results to all stakeholders, and they have asked you to complete a half-day training related to conflict/conflict resolution. In the space below, first articulate a rationale and overall description of your half-day training. Then use the template below to construct a training agenda related to conflict/conflict resolution.

TRAINING AGENDA

Content Summary: *Conflict Resolution*

_____

_____

_____

_____

_____

_____

Deliverables

Participants will:

- _____

- _____

- _____

- _____

9:00 a.m.	
9:15 a.m.	
9:30 a.m.	

(continued)

9:35 a.m.	
9:50 a.m.	
10:20 a.m.	
10:50 a.m.	
11:00 a.m.	
11:30 a.m.	

CHAPTER 14

External Communication Audits in a Digital World

As the global economy requires us to consider ongoing virtual operations, it is important for organizations to evolve in their digital communication efforts. This chapter will provide some important considerations when evaluating digital communication efforts.

Digital Communication

This book has generally dealt with internal communication—that is, communication that occurs within the organization. However, I do believe it is helpful to think strategically about how you communicate digitally both within and outside of the organization. As such, this chapter explores principles of a digital communication audit from an external communication perspective. Yet there are tangible principles that can be applied within an organization as well. This chapter strategically discusses the components that are involved when conducting a digital communication audit and then provides suggestions for putting an audit into practice.

Digital Presence

Organizations can, very literally, no longer afford to avoid a digital presence. In fact, it could be argued that almost every aspect, especially related to consumer behavior, has some sort of digital element. I consult often in the nonprofit realm, and the nonprofit sector is an interesting holistic case study for enhanced digital relations. Nonprofits must wrestle with the fact that donors now holistically prefer to give online and even more so through mobile tools, not necessarily a desktop or laptop. This translates to the corporate world. Customers, who may not even want to purchase online, expect an organization to have an online presence, and it is not enough to just "be" online. Instead, there should be active engagement with stakeholders through online means. An organization not only needs an outward facing digital presence but also needs a purposeful and intentional digital presence.

Internally, however, employees also expect efficient and effective technology to be used within the organization. Especially as organizations become younger, with more millennial and Generation Z employees, the technology expectations will increase (Strawser et al., 2021). It is imperative, then, that organizations have a streamlined communication plan that addresses digital elements.

Before going into each component of a digital communication audit, it is important to consider yet again the relationship between digital communication efforts and organizational ethos. Your organization's overarching goals, marketing goals, budget, and technology infrastructure will all (or should all) inform your digital strategy. Your digital strategy, then, influences how you use these outlets or platforms to engage with your own people and your external stakeholders. To think through these different elements, however, you need to go back to strategic goals.

Customer Experience Journey

A customer experience journey represents all of the experiences that a customer goes through as they interact with a company. Practically, this includes how and when a customer interacts with an organization. Digitally, customers can have multiple touch points with a brand or company as they proceed through the actual process of becoming a customer. From an audit perspective, the customer experience journey includes the channels where interaction happens between the consumer and the organization as well as where this interaction occurs, or the spaces where this interaction occurs.

A customer experience analysis can be helpful when diagnosing where customer experience may be poor compared to other interactions. Generally, when conducting a customer experience analysis, you should focus on direct interaction between the customer and the brand as well as any indirect interaction. Direct contact occurs when the customer and the organization interact via advertising, marketing, sales, and support. On the other hand, indirect contact is less formal and occurs through mentions of an organization, especially on social media, reviews, and word of mouth. Your analysis of a customer experience journey, then, can be structured similarly to a communication audit. You are trying to determine how interaction occurs and how effective this interaction is in achieving strategic goals.

If you do conduct a customer experience analysis, you can strategically analyze your website and other digital platforms. In addition, you can focus on the digital efforts of your competition and see what others in your industry are doing to interact with customers. Just like in a communication audit space, surveys that strategically ask customers to record their experiences with your brand can be extremely valuable.

The content above focuses on external realities: dealing with external customers or stakeholders. However, I do believe that approaching your employees as "customers" can be a great perspective. Internal communication should have a customer-centric element. Instead of thinking solely about your employees as information conduits, you can approach your overall communication plan similarly to how you would for your actual customers or clients. As you think about your communication audit from a digital perspective, imagine how your employees journey through their interactions with others within the organization.

Questions to Consider

1. Do employees have a centralized portal?

2. If a portal does exist, is it user-friendly (i.e., easy to navigate)?

3. Have you identified a communication process for your employees for human resources questions, training, and development, filing a report, and so forth?

4. Are your employees confused by any communication processes that exist within your organization?

Social Media Assessment

Organizations use social media platforms differently, obviously, but no matter how these tools are used, if a company does subscribe to a social media format for customer engagement, then an analysis is necessary. Social media assessment should begin first and foremost with a clear determination of key performance indicators. Before you can actually assess your social platforms, you should know exactly what would constitute success.

When I am asked to complete external communication audits, my clients will often ask me to also look at their social media interaction. I usually say yes, but I preface that answer with a reminder that social media is not a panacea; it is one tool in the toolbox. Unfortunately, because of the easy access and high potential, social media has become a low-hanging fruit for most organizations. If not approached intentionally, social platforms can waste substantial time and money. A social media audit or assessment can help organizations by focusing time, energy, and resources.

Before beginning a social assessment, you need to consider your end goals. Are you trying to just determine an evaluative understanding (i.e., whether something is working), or are you trying to actually establish new action steps that will help you be more effective? An assessment is evaluative, and an audit will lead to new implementation and demands action.

To conduct a social media assessment or audit, you need to follow a logical process.

- **Key performance indicators:** Key performance indicators (KPIs) are measurable metrics that can be used when evaluating social media performance. Your key performance indicators help you know which numbers to track. Your KPIs can measure a few different concepts: reach, including social impressions, follower count, audience growth rate, the number of people who have seen a post since it went live, potential reach (the number of people who could see a post), and social share of voice (the number of people mentioning your organization); engagement (likes, comments, positive interactions, average engagement rate, and amplification rate); and conversion (the number of people who perform actions defined in your social posts, number of people who click on the call to action, or bounce rate, which includes the number of people who made it to your site and then left quickly); and customer satisfaction (reviews and testimonials). By focusing your KPIs on reach, engagement, conversion, and satisfaction, you can strategically identify how your platforms are performing in relation to tangible and measurable concepts.

- **Inventory:** Once you determine your KPIs, you need to collect your social content. It may sound easy to collect all existing social media profiles, but it can be difficult. Your organization may exist in places where you do not have much of a following or where you have not actively pursued social engagement. This is an inventory step: Figure out where the organization exists in the social space.

- **Consistency:** Your social platforms should be analyzed for brand consistency. Is there a similar tone, language, color scheme, and ethos present for each platform that refers back to the organization at large?

- **Content:** Hopefully, you already have some sort of presence. As you go through the inventory list of all your platforms, identify your most successful content according to your predetermined KPIs. Track those key numbers across your content that has been performing the best. What themes and similarities are shared across the content you have posted?

- **Competition:** You can gain significant knowledge by analyzing the social platforms of the competition in the industry. What are organizations and companies doing in your similar space to engage audiences and customers online? Are there different ideas that seem to be working best for others? If so, what can you adopt and improve on at your organization?

These five steps—KPIs, inventory, consistency, content, and competition—may not solve all of your social media challenges, but they will help establish clarity for how to move forward. While social platforms are typically viewed as external mechanisms, there are organizations that use social media tools for internal communication purposes. The goals, while they are not identical, have a similar thread. If you use social media at your organization to reach your employees, you need to think about KPIs and how social fits into the broader communication strategy of your organization. Are you flooding your people with too much information and social is just an additional filler to an already messy situation, or have you used social platforms as an integral part of your overall internal strategy? Consider the five ideas before moving forward with an internal social strategy.

Social media can be useful internally. You can use it to promote organizational culture, build relationships, and share information. However, if social is a foundational element of your internal strategy, consider creating a social media policy that addresses external and internal issues, and make sure your people understand the point and purpose of the internal social strategy.

Storytelling

Digital efforts, especially external digital messages where stakeholders are involved in connecting with the brand, should have a framework that people can resonate with. When evaluating digital efforts, I appreciate a perspective that focuses on storytelling. Digital storytelling is just one method of delivering information to the audience, but it can be extremely effective. Storytelling as a marketing strategy uses narrative to communicate a message. Organizations should focus on storytelling in their marketing efforts when they want to communicate the narrative of their organization. Digital storytelling just uses computers and other multimedia elements to communicate a story to an audience. The focus is the same; the platform is just different. No matter how you are communicating stories, the best stories focus on people: the people you serve and the people who are part of your organization.

There are certainly other frameworks you can use to assess the effectiveness of digital messaging; however, storytelling provides a people-centric model. When analyzing digital storytelling efforts, focus on these concepts:

1. Have you articulated the main point and purpose of your story/storytelling efforts?

2. Have you developed a story that has reach and is accessible to your target audience?

3. Do your efforts utilize digital platforms effectively?

4. Have you created an aesthetically appealing product?

5. Have you focused on the right social platform to distribute your message?

Digital storytelling can be an exceptionally powerful mechanism for communicating with your target audience outside of your organization. Thankfully, it will also resonate internally. Employees want to be reminded of the organization's vision. As such, using digital storytelling mechanisms to draw in your own people can be helpful as you remind them of the underlying why: why your organization exists, how it helps people or serves clients, and what the true impact of your organization is and can be. The main goal here, though, is to identify and solidify a consistent framework that guides your messaging, both internally and externally.

Search Engine Optimization

When reviewing digital components, organizations would do well to establish a protocol for reviewing website content. Search engine optimization (SEO) can help organizations be more accessible, specifically to Google Search. I always view an organization's website as its digital hub. When I consult, I encourage clients to think about how they are guiding users and consumers back to their website and, even more specifically, what action steps they want their users to take. In my opinion, social media, email, blogs, and video/audio content should all bring people back to the website where they can engage more holistically with the brand. I know, however, that there are some who may disagree with that opinion.

Those who engage in SEO can make small modifications to their organization's website that will make it more recognizable to Google Search. SEO is all about helping search engines understand and present your content to searchers. You do not need an SEO expert to handle your website, but you should at the very least have someone on staff who is conversant with SEO. With that said, SEO is unfortunately changing daily, and it can be hard to keep up with new trends.

A communication audit can help organizations with a quick review of their SEO components. If a client wants my help analyzing their digital communications, specifically an external-facing website, I tend to focus on a general review of the site's structure and regular content, the organization's content development, and keyword research. There are certainly other elements you can focus on, but I find those categorizations to be most helpful as a baseline.

Generally, you need to help Google find your content, help Google understand your content, and optimize your site for keyword searches that will connect users to your organization. If you are interested, there are several SEO certifications that are available.

Search Engine Marketing

Similar to search engine optimization, search engine marketing (SEM) can help increase the visibility of your website in search engine results pages. SEO is focused on optimizing a website to get people to visit your website from organic web searchers, and SEM focuses on getting traffic from paid searches. When

SEM is a part of a digital strategy, the organization will use paid elements to increase search visibility; specifically, brands will pay for ads to appear as search results on search engine results pages. Like SEO, if an organization is utilizing SEM, keywords are an important part of the strategy. After you select target keywords and a user searches for those terms, then the brand or organization is charged when a user clicks on the ad.

If you are consulting with an organization and SEM is a part of the future strategy, you can help by assessing their current efforts or even creating SEM campaigns from scratch. If you are working with an organization without a SEM strategy, follow these steps initially:

- Conduct keyword research and select keywords that are relevant to the organization's website.

- Determine where (in terms of a geographic location) the add should be displayed.

- Create a text ad to display in the search results.

- Bid on the price the organization is willing to pay per click.

For both SEO and SEM, there is more involved than just the information listed above. Like SEO, there are SEM certifications and professional development courses available. No matter how involved you are in digital efforts as an internal or external communication professional, it is worth having a conversational knowledge of both SEO and SEM.

Moving Forward With a Digital Strategy

There probably could (and should) be a separate volume specifically on conducting a digital communication audit. The premise can be extremely involved, and the different elements that need review are changing constantly. This consistently moving target makes it hard to analyze and assess digital efforts. The addition of new technologies can also create challenges. With that said, organizations need to have a digital presence and their communication efforts should be supplemented, at the very least, with digital efforts. Digital communication cannot be ignored.

There are a few things organizations can do immediately to at least start the process of improving digital efforts.

- **Revisit or create a digital communication strategy:** This can be accomplished internally or externally, but it makes sense to have complementary strategies.

- **Know your audience:** Understand what your audience wants and needs. Again, this can be accomplished both internally and externally.

- **Establish a consistent brand tone and brand aesthetic:** Your organization's voice should be consistent, and the look of your digital platforms should be consistent as well.

- **Assess your current platforms:** Determine high- and low-performing platforms as well as content.

- **Involve people in the process:** Ask your audience what they need and want from your digital communication.

If this chapter is overwhelming, start small. If you tend to focus on communication that is not digital, then become conversant with digital efforts. Start to research new trends, build an expertise, and enhance your value.

ACTIVITIES AND DISCUSSION QUESTIONS

Briefly answer the following questions about your current (external) organizational digital presence.

Goals:

1. What are your current marketing goals (or the marketing goals of the organization you are auditing)?

_____

_____

_____

_____

_____

_____

2. What do you want or need to accomplish?

_____

_____

_____

_____

_____

_____

3. What are your digital strategy goals?

_____

_____

_____

_____

_____

_____

Strategy:

1. What is your current marketing strategy (or the marketing strategy of the organization you are auditing)?

_____

_____

_____

_____

_____

_____

2. What are your current strategic needs?

_____

_____

_____

_____

_____

_____

3. Where are the gaps in your approach?

_____

_____

_____

_____

_____

_____

Digital Strategy:

1. Can you easily describe the current online presence of your organization or the organization you are auditing?

_____

_____

_____

_____

_____

_____

2. What platforms have proven most effective for communicating, through digital channels, both inside and outside the organization?

_____

_____

_____

_____

_____

_____

WHAT WOULD YOU DO?

Imagine you have been asked by an organization to help rebrand their storytelling strategies. For purposes of this exercise, this can either be an organization you are currently connected to or an organization that you would like to pretend to give consulting tips. First, select a few organizations you think are great organizational storytellers (e.g., Disney). Second, research these organizations and determine how these exemplars are using story-telling techniques online. Third, create a mini executive summary for your organization. Offer practical suggestions for creating a more story-focused brand online.

_____

_____

_____

_____

_____

_____

_____

_____

_____

_____

CHAPTER 15

Putting It All Together

This chapter is unique in that it provides a summary of all previous chapters with several key takeaways from each chapter that will help to establish big picture audit clarity and synergy throughout the process.

Chapter Summaries and Big Ideas

CHAPTER 1:
WHAT IS A COMMUNICATION AUDIT,
AND WHY IS IT IMPORTANT?

By now, you should have a better understanding of exactly what a communication audit is and why we need to utilize this assessment tool in our organizations. Audits are, primarily, an evaluation tool. Because of this, audits can be helpful in solving communication-related problems in all types of organizations. One of the most important things to remember is that there should be a procedure or a process when conducting an audit. It does not mean that the audit does not change or that we cannot be flexible, but we can always adjust the audit format as long as the changes are purposeful and intentional. Before conducting an audit, think about the most pressing communication challenges in your organization and determine how the audit can be helpful for solving or identifying these issues. Audits are beneficial because they can increase communication consistency and efficiency, help you (or others) better understand and serve stakeholders, allow for organized communication efforts, and may foster an environment where communication overload can be minimized.

Chapter 1: Big Ideas

1. Use a communication audit to align communication efforts and organizational strategic goals.

2. Communication audits have a procedure: Be purposeful and intentional with what data you collect and why.

3. The audit can be helpful for establishing a bigger picture and data-driven communication strategy.

CHAPTER 2:
COMMUNICATION CONSULTING IN CONTEXT

While not always the case, communication audits can be used by internal or external communication consultants and can be a crucial tool in the consultant's toolbox. Consultants typically help organizations solve problems. A communication audit is primarily a problem-solving tool and, as such, can be a central service provided by a consultant. Consultants have many tasks but they specifically solve problems, recommend solutions, facilitate interventions, and evaluate outcomes. In the big picture, consultants can be influencers and change agents. As valuable organizational assets, consultants can provide unbiased insight in an ethical manner and can be a voice of reason. The sheer presence of a consultant may move the organization to make substantial changes, yet a consultant must, and can, do more than just be present. Instead, consultants can help pinpoint significant communication and relational challenges. For our purposes, the consultant is also a communicator and they can use communication audits to share their findings more effectively with clients or stakeholders.

Chapter 2: Big Ideas

1. Consultants can play a vital role in the health of an organization.

2. Communication audits can be a wonderful tool in the consultant's toolbox.

3. Consultants should be ethical organizational influencers and change agents: Providing data-driven suggestions to organizations can help consultants be ethical voices of change.

CHAPTER 3:
COMMUNICATION *IS* THE ORGANIZATION

Organizations consistently grow, evolve, and change. As such, they become sometimes more and sometimes less effective. It is important for us to remember that the central and defining characteristic of organizations is communication. Internal communication manifests itself in numerous capacities, and we must remember that all facets of the organization can be influenced, both positively and negatively, by communication. Audits provide valuable internal communication insights. Unfortunately, it is easy to feel overwhelmed by the sheer amount of information we receive on a regular basis and also the number of channels used to distribute this information. Audits can be used to assess both the communication preferences of members of the organization as well as the effectiveness of different organizational tools or platforms. Subsequently, communication audits can be used to develop an internal communication strategy that can focus on information sharing, best practices, diverse workforce considerations, and communication channels. If you use audits strategically, they can help make communication an organizational priority, achieve increased organizational and communication efficiency, unify voices, satisfy preferences, streamline channels, and allow for constructive dissent.

Chapter 3: Big Ideas

1. Communication *is* the organization.

2. Communication audits can help determine communication preferences and communication channel/platform efficiency.

3. Audits are useful for determining key components of an internal communication strategy.

CHAPTER 4:
DETERMINING THE PROCEDURE

Communication audits have a procedure and a process. They should not be approached without intentionality. Instead, those who conduct the audit must look at the holistic picture and strive to achieve some definitive process. Before determining the direction of the audit, you need to first understand organizational communication needs. The needs assessment can help you determine organizational shortcomings, but as you pursue an audit, you must think about three overarching questions: What do you need to measure, what do you want to measure, and what situational factors are influencing the organization? Once these questions are answered, you can begin the audit. The audit process framework starts with an initial consultation and planning meeting, then moves to a review of available resources. After this you would theoretically conduct a baseline needs assessment before collecting more in-depth data. After collecting data, you will analyze the data and then communicate results in a clear manner. This process can be repeated in almost any organizational setting. Underlying the audit process should be collaborative organizational goals.

Chapter 4: Big Ideas

1. Communication audits have a process.

2. Determine what you need to measure, what you want to measure, and any situational factors influencing the organization.

3. The audit process includes the initial consultation and planning meeting, review of resources, needs assessment, collecting data, analyzing data, and communicating results.

CHAPTER 5:
INVOLVING STAKEHOLDERS

You must involve stakeholders in the audit process. Stakeholders (i.e., those who have an interest in activities or decisions made by an organization) can include managers, executives, clients, and customers. Without buy-in from organizational stakeholders, an audit may return void. As you think about your stakeholders, determine their audit value, their potential level of involvement, communication that has already occurred with this individual/ department, and their potential receptiveness. To garner buy-in, consider having a discovery session where you find out initial stakeholder desires and be prepared to communicate an audit's value by giving a short elevator pitch for the audit tool. As the primary consultant in the audit process, you must be prepared to lead efficient and effective meetings with stakeholders. In addition, you should be prepared to observe meetings by looking at interactions between employees and employers, meeting processes and procedures (or lack thereof), as well as any meeting outcomes. Generally, you want to understand who needs to be involved in the process and at what capacity.

Chapter 5: Big Ideas

1. Involve key stakeholders throughout all phases of the audit process.

2. Garner buy-in by clearly communicating the audit's value propositions.

3. Be prepared to both lead and observe meetings with organizational stakeholders.

CHAPTER 6: THE PROCESS, STEP 1:
NEEDS ASSESSMENT

The needs assessment should be aligned with strategic organizational goals. The needs assessment is the first step in determining how to measure organizational data as it relates to communication effectiveness. The needs assessment provides crucial data related to gaps in organizational results. A needs assessment helps determine what *really is* compared to *what should be*. A needs assessment also shows you the direction for the remaining audit. The main purpose of the needs assessment is to help you, the auditor, determine where to focus the audit. There are different phases of the needs assessment. The pre-assessment phase relies on preexisting data; the second phase, the assessment itself, potentially establishes a causal analysis and even prioritization of needs; and the post-assessment phase is used to determine next steps. The needs assessment process as a more in-depth enterprise is concerned with information gathering, analysis, and determination of needs. There are different types of needs assessments, and this volume shares differences between training needs assessments, performance needs assessments, and organizational needs assessments.

Chapter 6: Big Ideas

1. Align the needs assessment with strategic organizational goals.

2. A needs assessment reveals what actually exists, while an audit can tell us what should be.

3. The needs assessment is focused on information gathering, analysis, and determination of needs.

CHAPTER 7: THE PROCESS, STEP 2: COLLECTING DATA AND METHODOLOGY

There are many different options for collecting data throughout the audit process. It may be that you need to use different methods depending on the situation. The data collection methods addressed in this chapter may be helpful as you strive to make data-driven suggestions for the organization. You may want to start with surveys, or questionnaires, that are helpful for collecting data at scale. There are different surveys you can use that are available at no cost, but you can also develop your own if you have specific questions that need to be addressed. A survey may incorporate either closed or open-ended questions. Some of my favorite surveys include the Communication Satisfaction

Questionnaire, the ICA Audit Survey, the Organizational Communication Development Audit Questionnaire, and the Organizational Communication Scale. Focus groups are also a viable option. Focus groups, unlike surveys, provide more in-depth information through interviewing a group of representatives from the organization. Focus groups can be valuable because you can hear how individuals respond to each other. Focus groups tend to include between five and seven individuals and should encourage participation from representative voices. Unlike focus groups, in-depth interviews provide valuable information because of the feedback by one specific individual at length. Interviews can be extremely personal but may be time consuming. A less popular data collection tool is the critical incident analysis. In a critical incident analysis, participants are asked to describe effective or ineffective communication experiences very specifically at their organization. Then the auditor would use this feedback to suggest a new (or similar) model for the future. Next, a network analysis is used to understand the entire communication flow or framework of an organization. Auditors here should look for connections between communication platforms, channels, and the holistic information exchange. Observation can be used to help you, the auditor, see different situations firsthand. Finally, a document review includes the analysis of past strategic or communication plans and subsequently finding valuable information within these documents.

Chapter 7: Big Ideas

1. Thoughtfully consider how data should be collected as you consider the strategic communication goals, specifically of the audit and the organization at large.

2. There are several different data collection methods: surveys, focus groups, in-depth interviews, critical incident analyses, network analyses, and observation.

3. You do not have to reinvent the wheel every time you collect data. Search for previous scales/measures, research different potential interview or focus group questions, and so on. Do not assume that you have to start with a completely blank slate.

CHAPTER 8: THE PROCESS, STEP 3: ANALYZING DATA AND CLARIFYING RESULTS

After you determine how you are going to collect your data, you need to then (obviously) collect the data. After data has been collected, you must analyze what you have. Data analysis does not have to be cumbersome and confusing. There are ways to approach data analysis that do not require substantial research methods training. There are several programs you can use, like Qualtrics, that allow you to determine mean, or average, scores on survey responses. In addition, when you are analyzing qualitative data, you can try to identify similarities or patterns of responses. Just remember you are trying to find the most applicable results.

Chapter 8: Big Ideas

1. Data analysis does not have to be complicated. Use the tools (and expertise) you have at your disposal.

2. Find software and platforms that you are comfortable using and continue using those platforms to become more proficient.

3. Find the most applicable results per your strategic communication audit goals.

CHAPTER 9: THE PROCESS, STEP 4: COMMUNICATING THE RESULTS

Data-driven recommendations are crucial if you want the audience to enact the audit and make changes based on your findings. However, along with this key component, it is just as important to note that how you communicate your results can have significant influence (both positive and negative) on whether or not change occurs. Many can collect data and even analyze data. If you are an internal or external communication consultant, you can have significant value to the organization if you subsequently communicate your findings in a clear and digestible way. This chapter provides 10 steps to effectively communicate your results: Review your promised deliverables, conduct an audience analysis, simplify your findings, offer explanations, share (simply), present visually, be timely, let data speak for itself, offer concrete recommendations, and include action items and next steps. Before communicating your results, mediate on your stakeholders and your initial objectives. Then begin the process of tailoring your message to your desired audience.

Chapter 9: Big Ideas

1. Tailor your message to your stakeholder audience.

2. Simplify your message to appeal to different stakeholders.

3. Present findings in a clear and simple manner, and vary your style when needed.

CHAPTER 10:
DEALING WITH RESULTS

Audits will never present *only* positive results. Instead, it is my experience that most audits reveal negative communication issues. These negative concerns may be related to personnel or may just show that different platforms are not working. There are several different reasons presented in this chapter that explain why an audit may go wrong. These issues include auditor bias, inaccurate results, insufficient data collection, suggesting the wrong fix, reporting results in jargon, confusion about the audit purpose, or assuming one problem and subsequently one solution. Before assuming that you need to share bad news, go back and make sure these audit challenges have been resolved. Once you determine that your information is correct and that the audit was completed sufficiently (and you still have bad news), you need to consider how you share this information. First, make sure you present your information directly; report the facts. Second, frame your findings within the broader context of the organization and remind your stakeholders that you are presenting your results. Third, in matters related to personnel, be as transparent as you need to be without mentioning names or individual employees when it is not necessary. Fourth, focus on the future and give stakeholders and opportunity to solve problems: Present future hope. You cannot escape presenting unflattering results but you can prepare. Make sure to rehearse and give opportunities for feedback.

Chapter 10: Big Ideas

1. Perform an audit check to make sure your results are correct and data collection measures were sufficient.

2. Present negative or difficult results directly, in a manner that is not personal and easy to understand.

3. Practice and rehearse how you communicate difficult results and also offer stakeholders the opportunity to offer feedback.

CHAPTER 11:
INTERNAL COMMUNICATION STRATEGY

A completed communication audit has numerous benefits, but chief among them may be the ability to use the audit to inform and develop an internal communication strategy. This chapter explored the process of developing an internal communication plan and provided steps for accomplishing this goal. The steps explored in this chapter include, first, establishing an end goal. Before developing the plan, you should articulate the vision for the internal strategy and determine what your internal communication strategy should accomplish. Second, your internal communication strategy should be evidence-based. This is where an audit can be helpful. The audit can be the primary way you gather your evidence to inform your communication strategy. Third, your internal communication efforts should be aligned with other organizational initiatives. Fourth, once you have accomplished Steps 1–3, you should then strategize and create an internal communication plan that is both attainable and implementable. As you move toward creating your internal strategy, set your objectives, determine the main messaging components (framing, narrative, etc.) that you want to emphasize, select appropriate channels or mediums where information can be transferred to preferred audiences, and finally determine message frequency. Remember that as you develop the initial strategy, you should encourage feedback from members of the organization and consider your strategy as a means to build relationships across the organization.

Chapter 11: Big Ideas

1. A holistic communication strategy is needed today more than ever.

2. Communication audits can inform your internal communication strategy.

3. Encourage buy-in from organizational stakeholders throughout the process.

CHAPTER 12:
INFUSING AN AUDIT INTO ORGANIZATIONAL CULTURE

Communication audits, if conducted effectively, can lead to widespread organizational change. While it may be difficult to pinpoint specifically what cultural issues exist in organizations, audits can at least provide data-driven observations as well as realistic places to begin to make holistic changes. This chapter addressed organizational culture through the lens of four different cultural distinctives: strategy, structure, relationships, and processes. Throughout the chapter, arguments were made as to (a) why audits can reveal organizational issues related to these four distinctives and, more importantly, (b) how audits can help solve some of these cultural problems. For an audit to be effective, stakeholders must buy into the premise and purpose of the audit and simultaneously be willing to implement suggestions revealed by the findings.

Chapter 12: Big Ideas

1. Communication audits can reveal issues with organizational culture.

2. There are four distinguishing factors of organizational culture: strategy, structure, people, and processes.

3. Communication audits, from the beginning of the process, must be framed as culture-identifying and culture-changing initiatives.

CHAPTER 13:
USING RESULTS TO INFORM
ORGANIZATIONAL TRAINING

Organizational training should not just be a box to check. Audits can be helpful because they reveal training needs and can help the auditor develop appropriate training curriculum. There are many different communication topics that can be addressed in a training context, and this chapter specifically mentioned presentation skills, team skills, and interpersonal skills. The role of the communication trainer is that of both subject matter expert and trainer. As such, when designing and facilitating communication training, the communication trainer should focus the training on the needs of the client. The goal, like all consulting elements, should be to enact organizational change. The National Communication Association has released a best practices list for communication training. The list includes the following best practices: Maintain transparency to clients and trustees, use accessible methods, demonstrate technology proficiency, demonstrate professional development, develop and maintain organizational expertise, demonstrate effective and appropriate instructional design, and demonstrate communication proficiency. Finally, a needs-centered training model was presented as a potential exemplar when thinking about communication training design and facilitation.

Chapter 13: Big Ideas

1. Training should be needs-centered, results-informed, and purposeful.

2. Training should be procedural, and progress and should start when employees are onboarded.

3. A communication trainer should be an effective communicator and must have effective presentation skills, relational skills, and group facilitation skills.

CHAPTER 14:
EXTERNAL COMMUNICATION
AUDITS IN A DIGITAL WORLD

This book has primarily focused on internal communication assessment. Often, audits will help identify gaps in communication that occur within the organization. However, as this chapter illustrated, we cannot forsake external communication, and much of our external communication occurs in an online space. This chapter explores ways to assess digital presence. An organization's overarching goals, marketing goals, budget, and technology infrastructure will all inform digital strategy. There were several questions posed in the chapter that can help evaluate an organization's digital strategy. The questions focus on goals, strategy, and, more specifically, digital strategy. The chapter content suggests starting first with the customer experience journey and determining all of the touch points an individual customer or client has with your organization. From there, information regarding social media assessments and the evaluation of specific platforms and strategies is provided. The following process was provided for conducting a social media assessment: (1) Determine key performance indicators, (2) determine inventory, (3) evaluate consistency, (4) evaluate content, and (5) review what the competition is doing. As a framework for external messaging, storytelling was detailed as a methodological and customer-centered process. Finally, information was provided for making a website that is search engine friendly both through optimization and marketing.

Chapter 14: Big Ideas

1. If your organization does not have one, it is time to create or revisit the topic of a digital strategy.

2. Just like when dealing with internal communication, know your audience and understand their wants and needs.

3. Establish a consistent brand aesthetic through all of your digital platforms.

APPENDIX A ──────────────

Industry Voices

Two experienced professionals were asked to provide advice for internal communication strategy. Performance Improvement Strategist Caitlin Johnson provides four key considerations related to identifying meaningful goals and Scott Bennett, Director, Global Quality Assurance Communications, reminds you to listen before you speak. The advice in this appendix comes from years of practical experience. Their insights are valuable and helpful!

Identifying Meaningful Goals

Caitlin Johnson, Performance Improvement Strategist

At the beginning of a strategic goal-setting conversation, it may feel as if there are endless possibilities to focus on. To develop meaningful goals, it's important to take into account key considerations that will inform what needs to be measured and tracked. Additionally, if a behavior change is needed from the team and the organization, it's important to have a goal that engages rational business components as well as engages an emotional personal component as well.

FOUR KEY CONSIDERATIONS IN
IDENTIFYING MEANINGFUL GOALS

1. **Identify ways in which the communications team can bring value to the organization.**

   Host a brainstorming session to gather the communication team to think through all the ways the team can bring value.

   Consider the rational components. In essence, what are the results the organization is looking for the communication team to deliver? While it is important to drive results, it's critical to align results to a bigger purpose.

   Consider the emotional components. What motivates and drives the communication team forward: Is it because they know the impact of their work provides a bigger sense of meaning and purpose? Consider the "what's in it for me" (WIIFM) and the why behind the goal. When you can align a business goal to a personal connection, the personal investment of achieving the goal significantly increases.

   During the brainstorm session, consider answering the following questions:

   - What opportunities exist that the communication team could focus on to make an impact? If the organization has an associate review, analyze any feedback to glean ideas.

   - Based on the organization's culture, what is the value of the communication team? How can the team showcase that value?

   - What is the sense of purpose the individuals of the communication team feel they bring to the organization? How can that be aligned to business results?

   - What is a key differentiator of the communication team? How can the team make a difference through communication and stand out as a value-add department?

   Examples: Ensure effective communications by incorporating the "why" to help employees understand organizational intent, sending communications in a timelier manner, developing a consistent cadence of communication, improving employee engagement through clear and concise communication, identifying ways to be proactive in understanding communication needs, developing better relationships with stakeholders to have a seat at the table, and so on.

2. **Narrow the focus on the *epically* important.**

Once the brainstorming list has been compiled, narrow down the brainstorm to the top five focus items. Next, identify what is the one most epically important goal to focus on.

To identify the epically important, answer this question: Based on these top five focus areas, which do we feel like if we do not achieve by the end of the year, all other efforts will feel inconsequential?

Be mindful of the law of diminishing returns, which states the more items we focus on, the less likely each item will be achieved. When there is more than one goal, time must be split to achieve results, therefore diluting efforts to achieve the items identified.

Land on a goal that motivates and engages the team to produce results. The goal should feel meaningful, demonstrate value, and clearly describe intent.

3. **Write the goal in a crystal clear and structured format.**

Goals that are not written down are just hopeful visions. If the goal is not written, it can be quickly forgotten. Writing a clear goal that includes a timeframe, a starting point, and an ending point helps a team be crystal clear on the direction.

When finalizing the goal:

- Determine the time frame or deadline for when you want to achieve the goal: Is it a project goal that has a specific end date? Is it an annual goal to be completed by December 31?

- Determine the starting point by identifying the current state: Are you starting from scratch? Is there a metric that you are looking to increase? Use the current score of the metric you are looking to increase as the starting point.

- Determine the ending point by determining how much you want to increase or improve: Be realistic with the target ending point, as the goal needs to be achievable and motivational. Develop a winnable goal. Consider cutting the target goal in half. If the team achieves it relatively quickly, celebrate the results and then determine a stretch goal. Keep the momentum going. It's better to develop a stretch goal and stay motivated versus not reaching the goal at all.

Goals that measure something you can see help sustain motivation and desire. Whenever possible, consider using numbers rather than percentages.

4. **Communicate the progress on the goal consistently and often.**

   Once a goal has been identified, progress on the goal must be discussed on a weekly basis. Be consistent. Without consistency, the goal will fall to the side as unimportant, and the perception will become a "flavor of the week" mentality. Through repetition, the momentum behind goal achievement is reinforced and sustained.

   To support clear communication around the progress of the goal, develop a tracker, scoreboard, or dashboard to show the progress to the team. This can be a simple visual to help the team see the value of their efforts in gaining traction on the goal.

   The benefits of having a scoreboard:

   - It reinforces the importance of the team's efforts and the value of the department.

   - It rallies the team around making a continued impact and holds the team accountable for results.

   - It helps provide feedback to the team on their efforts. Are the efforts driving the score? Should the team keep going or does the team need to revisit the execution strategy?

Listen Before You Speak—Always

Scott Bennett, Director, Global Quality Assurance Communications at P&G

We tend to associate communications with the *dissemination* of a message, with varying levels of accuracy or targeting to reach a specific audience(s). As communicators, we often feel the compulsion to always be sending out something—anything—to justify our worth and existence. But communication is as much (if not more) about receiving information as it is about sending it.

As a professional writing major in college, I had it drilled into my brain that intentional listening must always bathe any communication or messaging strategy. You can call it "sensing" or "audience analysis" or "focus groups" or "surveys" or a "landscape assessment," but without some type of listening or input exercise to understand those who will experience your communications (including their beliefs, aspirations, fears, expectations, and backstories), your best communication outputs into a vacuum will be tone deaf at best and could permanently erode people's trust at worst.

Lastly, listening is not a one-and-done endeavour. We must be constantly trolling the waters to immerse ourselves in the current conversations that are happening, the temperature of the room, the trends that are spiking at any given time, and the top news stories to ensure that what we drop into the ocean of chatter strikes the right chord at the right time.

MAJOR ON THE "WHY"

So much we have to communicate deals with the minutiae of a change, or a new initiative: "We're changing to a new software program. It will replace a host of outdated software programs we currently use. Here is a link to the training. The training will take you approximately 1 hour to complete. Take the training by such-and-such a date."

This is all critical information to communicate to your audience. But these are human beings we're dealing with. They're not robots. They have families. They have favorite foods and favorite colors. They have hobbies and interests.

Human beings, unlike any other living thing on Earth, certainly appreciate knowing the "what" and the "when." But they are most deeply motivated and animated by the "why." They will only go so far just knowing the what and when.

But if you take away their why, they opt out. Or to put it positively, if you give them a meaningful and principled why, they're all in.

Sometimes this requires painting a picture for them of the end state: "Imagine being able to do all of your daily tasks in one software program—and in a fraction of the time." Sometimes it requires laddering it up to a higher purpose: "This new software program is just one key building block of a larger strategy the company is undertaking." Sometimes it requires storytelling to bring the why to life: "Location X just completed its cutover to the new software program, and here's what Dave in accounting has to say about it."

In your diligence to clearly communicate next steps and timings as it relates to a change or initiative, which is critically important, let's not forget to consistently reinforce the why—not just once but at each step of the way—because the why is something our brains crave in order to fully invest, to bust through barriers, and to see something all the way to completion.

GET COMFORTABLE LIVING IN A FISHBOWL

The 21st century has opened up the floodgates of open "surround-sound" communication between brands and their consumers, between companies and their employees, between politicians and their constituents, between churches and their parishioners, between organizations and their donors, between media channels and their viewers, and so on. There is no longer a veil that entities can hide behind, or a hole they can crawl into, if they're being pelted with pressure, complaints, or accusations.

Transparency is an unavoidable feature of today's communication professional. The public forums that now provide unprecedented freedom for individuals to communicate with stalwart entities require brands, companies, politicians, churches, and organizations to be far more prepared to engage on any topic that may come up. If you can't stand the heat, get out of the kitchen.

STUDY THE GREATS

We are all surrounded by terrible communications, from billboards that you don't have time to read, to spam email from companies that obviously bought your email address from an identity thief, to paper junk mail that looks like a third-grader created it, to 90-second TV commercials for drugs that don't even tell you what disease they treat.

Bad communications are everywhere. But great communications are too. And as communicators, we need to be connoisseurs of best-in-class communications, which means we need to proactively offset and combat the barrage of bad communications coming at us by surrounding ourselves with that which inspires us. And there is plenty out there! You just have to look a little harder for it. And I would recommend starting with just one. Whether it's a podcast, an e-newsletter, a documentary, or a YouTube channel, there is amazing content out there to consume, but it's probably not going to beat down your door like bad communications do. You have to go out and find it.

I find that the more I immerse myself and surround myself with inspiring communications, the stronger my own communications get, day by day.

One of the people whose work I get inspired by is Ira Glass, who hosts a number of award-winning podcasts for NPR, including *This American Life*. He talks about the discipline of communications (or as he calls it, storytelling) as a practice that we never perfect. All we can do is try to make the next thing we do better than the last thing we did. And you will. Then when you look back on something you did a year ago, you'll say, "Oh, that was so bad." And that's OK! We're all somewhere on the continuum. And there's no shame in studying (and even emulating) what you find to be inspiring and well executed and reapplying aspects of it when you go to develop a strategy for whatever it is you need to communicate. There's no shame in that.

CREATE A DISRUPTION

Whether we like to admit it or not, communications professionals are in the disruption business. And please know that I'm using the word "disruption" in a constructive light.

As communicators, we are swimming against a tsunami of competing messages with every message we send. Our only hope for success rests in whether we find a way to rise above it—or as I like to say, **zig when the rest of the world is zagging**.

We've all received that spam email or seen that YouTube ad that just stopped us in our tracks. Some manage to do that. What was it about it that captivated me? Something about it was disruptive. It grabbed me by the chin and whirled me around to pay attention. That is not accidental, it is not common, and it is not easy.

So always be thinking, "How can I create a disruption with this message?" not in a deceptive or inappropriate way, but in a constructive way. Sometimes that is an arresting visual. Sometimes it is the subject line of an email message that is offbeat. Sometimes it is an overabundance of white space, when everything else looks cluttered.

Simplicity and brevity are some of the most powerful tools of disruption we can use because most of what we see out there tends to be so wordy. The absence of complexity and verbosity can be oddly disruptive in our culture. So think about how your message can zig when others zag, and create a disruption.

ELEVATE VOICES BESIDES YOUR OWN

In the early 2000s, a new term emerged in communications called "influencers." But the use of influencers was not a new idea then. Forty years before that, we had Mr. Whipple the store clerk telling customers not to squeeze the Charmin and Rosey the waitress swearing by Bounty, the Quicker Picker Upper.

But as we entered the 21st century, a string of corporate corruption and scandals caused consumers to develop a healthy suspicion toward brands, or the companies behind them, telling us what we needed. We naturally question the motives of a brand or company. We'd sooner believe the advice of a dermatologist or a dentist, an athlete, or even an engineer or a technical expert on the topic pertaining to the product.

So companies and brands started enlisting these trustworthy voices as paid spokespeople, or influencers, to speak for them. And we see these ads every day: football players promoting razors, models promoting shampoo, and frontline workers promoting sanitizing spray.

Get in the habit of asking yourself, "Who are the most trustworthy voices on this topic?" Sometimes it is a senior leader. But sometimes it is the testimonial of someone in the trenches who can speak the language of your audience—someone they can really relate to.

Think about what voices in your organization matter most and how you can elevate them in your communications to help inform and inspire the organization to embrace and adopt a change or an initiative. Maybe you use a quote from them. Maybe you set up a call and invite them to present their perspective to the organization. There are a number of ways to incorporate other voices into your communications. The most important thing is that you're elevating them!

APPENDIX B ———————————————

Final Evaluation Report

Organizational Efficiency and Employee Engagement Report

LEGACY
COMMUNICATION

EXECUTIVE SUMMARY

Legacy Communication Training and Consulting, LLC, was engaged to assess communication effectiveness and efficiency. To engage the entire employee base as well as gather a deeper understanding of opportunities and strengths, a two-pronged approach of online survey and in-person interviews was established. As a result, the project was completed in two phases.

Phase 1 included an online survey and communication platform review. Phase 2 involved face-to-face interviews with staff at various levels of the organization to verify the information and trends identified in the survey.

Overall, the process revealed several areas with opportunity for improvement. While, overall, employees feel positive about the work they are doing and the general means by which communication occurs, there is a general lack of trust between staff and supervisors. A lack of clarity about roles and responsibilities as well as difficulty navigating change appear to be the greatest communication challenges. Additionally, there are tensions between cohort groups based on job functions. This could stem from the larger issue of roles and responsibilities and some groups feeling that they work harder or are less recognized for their work than other groups.

Recommendations for next steps are included in the report to address many of the issues identified.

Survey Results

The survey was completed with 36 employees. The 43 questions assessed several key areas, including communication satisfaction, engagement, professional growth/career advancement, job training, application of talent and skills, adaptability and flexibility of coworkers, compensation, and job satisfaction. The measurement for Likert Scale responses was based on a 5-point scale with "agree" to "strongly agree" being considered positive and "neutral" or below considered negative. The evaluator considered "90% agree" or "strongly agree" to be the goal and below that to be an opportunity area. The data was analyzed both overall and by cohort group to identify trends and challenges to be addressed.

SURVEY COMPLETION PARTICIPANT DEPARTMENT REPRESENTATION:

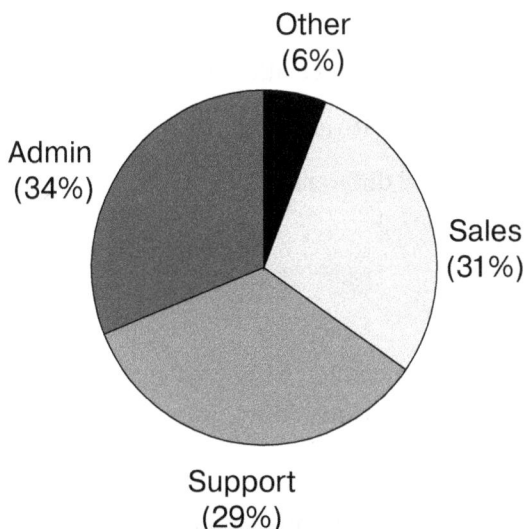

| FIG A.1 Particpation by Department

ONE-ON-ONE INTERVIEWS

Over the course of 2 business days, 16 in-depth interviews were conducted with representative employees. Questions focused on overall culture, leadership, as well as communication style and expectations. Several themes emerged from these interviews, including but not limited to:

The interview responses were generally thoughtful. The evaluator did notice that many respondents were nervous, even anxious, throughout their session. However, this could be explained by the presence of the consultant. The interviews did reveal several essential realities and reinforced much of what was discussed in the survey.

THEMES

Quotes were selected to reinforce represented themes. It should be noted that not every interviewee necessarily had identical feelings, but a consensus was identified for all the themes below. In addition, to avoid quotes being taken out of context, we provided context where appropriate.

Strengths Identified

1. There is a sense of loyalty and deep appreciation for employees.
2. Interviewees enjoy overall atmosphere and enjoy their coworkers.
3. There are significant generational differences.
4. Leadership is mission driven.

Challenges Identified

1. There is a lack of clear organizational structure.
2. There is a lack of accountability/inconsistent accountability.
3. There are inconsistent job expectations and responsibilities.
4. There is a general lack of professionalism.
5. There is a lack of clarity regarding the purpose of certain positions.
6. Some jobs are viewed as "beneath" certain employees.
7. There are significant job description overlaps.
8. There needs to be recognition when jobs are not being accomplished.
9. There is tension between front of building and back of building.
10. There is some tension between longer tenured staff and newer staff.
11. Communication is inconsistent and confusing

The themes revealed in the interviews are not uncommon. Typically, the supervisor bears the brunt of organizational and communication inefficiency and needs more support. There are, however, several underlying issues that are concerning. For one—and this was not represented in the themes—a common finding was that the newer hires are unsure of what expectations the company has of them. This is not sustainable. Also, there is a general lack of accountability as well as inconsistent accountability, and the workers notice. In addition, there is a lack of clarity regarding what some members of the organization do and what they are responsible for doing. An implication of this is that messaging has been identified as distorted and unhelpful. Again, what is most concerning here is that employees notice this inconsistency. Finally, tensions do exist that, if not addressed soon, could lead to significant issues in the future.

RECOMMENDATIONS

Our recommendations center on three areas: a streamlined communication plan, increasing accountability, and organizational culture.

COMMUNICATION PLAN

1. The organization should incorporate a new communication plan. Specifically, there should be a streamlined focus as the organization considers what messages are sent and from where (i.e., format and frequency). In addition, we recommend that the organization create a communication flowchart that focuses on consistent messages and most appropriate platform.

ACCOUNTABILITY

2. The organization should revise existing job descriptions and collaborate with employees regarding these streamlined expectations. It is then recommended that management evaluate each member of the team to ensure that they are currently filling the role that best suits their talents and strengths. We can provide an evaluation tool to ensure each staff member is in the "right seat on the bus."

ORGANIZATIONAL CULTURE

3. A plan should be developed to increase communication both within teams and across teams to build a better understanding of job responsibilities.

4. Any employee recognition program should ensure that one team is not being favored over other teams.

5. Since "change management" was identified as a significant stressor, managers should be trained on how to better communicate and reduce stress during times where operations need to shift quickly. This is not an innate skill and can be taught to improve the impact of change on staff.

6. While staff love the work they do and the impact it has, creating a culture of respect and collaboration takes work. Creating a culture chart for how everyone should be treated will help build a positive environment for everyone. Using a culture chart of behaviors desired to then hire and coach the team will help to ensure they are using emotional intelligence when they interact with others.

MOVING FORWARD

We believe these recommendations will help your organization achieve continued success. If you would like to engage us in future endeavors, we can help. If needed, we can provide support through the next 6 months if you decide to create a new organizational structure and job descriptions. In addition, we would be happy to provide coaching/training to supervisors.

Survey Results

Question	Strongly disagree	Disagree	Neutral	Agree	Strongly agree	90% threshold met
I am satisfied with my opportunities for professional growth.	6%	3%	30%	39%	21%	No
My organization is dedicated to my professional development.	0%	9%	33%	39%	18%	No
I am satisfied with the job-related training my organization offers.	0%	9%	41%	38%	12%	No
I get excited about going to work.	3%	3%	24%	42%	27%	No
I am inspired to meet my goals at work.	3%	6%	9%	52%	30%	No
I feel completely involved in my work.	0%	3%	9%	48%	39%	No
I am often so involved in my work that the day goes by very quickly.	0%	3%	15%	61%	21%	No
I am determined to give my best effort at work each day.	3%	0%	3%	36%	58%	Yes
When at work, I am completely focused on my job duties.	0%	3%	9%	48%	39%	No
In my organization, employees adapt quickly to difficult situations.	0%	9%	15%	52%	24%	No

(continued)

Question	Strongly disagree	Disagree	Neutral	Agree	Strongly agree	90% threshold met
In my organization, supervisors adapt quickly to difficult situations.	0%	6%	15%	55%	24%	No
Employees here always keep going when the going gets tough.	0%	13%	6%	50%	31%	No
Supervisors here always keep going when the going gets tough.	0%	3%	9%	63%	25%	No
Employees proactively identify future challenges and opportunities.	3%	0%	40%	53%	3%	No
Employees in my organization take the initiative to help other employees when the need arises.	0%	9%	19%	53%	19%	No
Employees here are willing to take on new tasks as needed.	0%	9%	16%	60%	16%	No
Employees in my organization willingly accept change.	0%	9%	44%	41%	6%	No
Communication between supervisors and employees is good in my organization.	6%	9%	31%	41%	13%	No
I am able to make decisions affecting my work.	0%	6%	9%	63%	22%	No

Question	Strongly disagree	Disagree	Neutral	Agree	Strongly agree	90% threshold met
Management within my organization recognizes strong job performance.	3%	9%	22%	56%	9%	No
My supervisor and I have a good working relationship.	3%	0%	6%	53%	38%	Yes
My coworkers and I have a good working relationship.	0%	3%	9%	50%	38%	No
Supervisors and employees trust each other.	3%	16%	25%	34%	22%	No
Employees treat each other with respect.	6%	3%	18%	64%	9%	No
My organization has a safe work environment.	0%	0%	6%	58%	35%	Yes
I am satisfied with my overall job security.	0%	3%	10%	61%	26%	No
My organization's work positively impacts people's lives.	3%	0%	6%	26%	65%	Yes
My organization operates in a socially responsible manner.	0%	0%	10%	45%	45%	Yes
My organization's fiscal well-being is stable.	0%	0%	23%	55%	23%	No
I understand how my work impacts the organization's business goals.	0%	0%	10%	52%	39%	Yes

(*continued*)

Question	Strongly disagree	Disagree	Neutral	Agree	Strongly agree	90% threshold met
My organization is dedicated to diversity and inclusiveness.	6%	6%	10%	55%	23%	No
I am satisfied with the culture of my workplace.	0%	3%	19%	55%	23%	No

Question	Extremely well	Very well	Somewhat well	Not so well	Not at all well	90% threshold met
How well did the job duties you were given match your knowledge and skills?	29%	58%	10%	0%	3%	No

Question	1	2	3	4	5	90% threshold met
Rate your job performance on a scale of 1 to 5, with 1 being poor and 5 being exceptional.	0%	3%	3%	59%	34%	Yes

OPEN-ENDED QUESTION

One open-ended question was asked at the end of the survey. Employees were asked, "If you were in charge, what changes would you make to the organization?" Select responses are included below.

"More communication with upper management and the regular employees."

"Hold senior staff accountable for their job duties. Many duties are not being completed and affect other staff. Get rid of staff who are content and have a toxic attitude (always argumentative with fellow coworkers, always negative to suggestions). Overall, more organized/set job responsibilities. Management staff should be doing their jobs and it shouldn't have to fall on the [the leader] who works well over 50 hours a week putting out fires. Entry level staff shouldn't have to make up the slack for senior staff refusing to do duties."

"There would be communication changes and clarity on new tasks assigned."

"Everyone would have checks and balances to ensure that individuals are completing their daily tasks. All work would also be distributed evenly."

"Better communication. Communication. Communication. Clear and concise jobs, usually too many hands working on things when it should be less. Not everyone needs to know everything about everything. Consistency in discipline; just because someone is doing something, doesn't mean we all should be punished."

"More communication between supervisors and employees and I would take the time to listen to employee suggestions and ask for employee's ideas and help before initiating a new order. Changes are made without consulting the employees that do the work to see if the change will work or can be made better."

"I would just say to have better communication overall."

"The direct supervisor should be the one I have to speak with on daily basis. Too many times others are coming in (and) interfering or trying to overrule my direct supervisor. VERY UNPROFESSIONAL."

"That there would be more interaction between employees and the people that work higher up."

SELECT INTERVIEW QUOTES AND THEMES

REPRESENTED NEGATIVE THEMES

1. There is a lack of clear organizational structure.

Sample quotes:

"I don't want to be negative, but I think that [overall structure] is lacking and I think that leads to a hazy understanding."

2. There is a lack of accountability/inconsistent accountability.

Sample quotes:

"But it's, you know, (some) may be treated differently. ... You may know you have been mistreated or treated differently than others; it's like you know everybody's on a different kind of pedestal, and I don't think that's right."

"It's just that, there's kind of a lack of accountability. ... It's just that sometimes employees might [get] lazy."

"The morale needs to be improved because some people, let's just say they can walk on water."

"This is the first job I've ever had that doesn't do that structure [of weekly reports] and I don't know how weekly reports fit into this culture. ... Maybe if there's a one-on-one report sheet that you prepare whether it's once a week. ..."

"[Communication issues exist] and it's like, hey, do this, because someone is not doing their job."

"[I believe] they [leadership] are aware of who will get the work done and who will do it properly, and who will not, and I think there's ample opportunity for people to get things done, and a lot of the times it's just not. But I think there should be a system of checks and balances. I think there should be a list of things that people are supposed to be doing ... and there should be actions taken, or some sort of consequence ... because I think there's a lack of motivation."

[When asked if work is evenly distributed] "I do not, simply because of accountability, and then when things fall off the wagon that way, that falls to [the leader], and he has way more responsibility than he should ever have."

3. **There are inconsistent job expectations and responsibilities.**

Sample quotes:

"We have events. I would like to see more planning. And kind of practically what is needed from everyone."

"It is kind of blurry as to what I'm doing."

"[There are sometimes] no actual set guidelines."

[Re: what changes would you make to the organization] "I'm definitely giving people job descriptions or tasks that actually fit what they need to be doing ... because again certain tasks should be lumped into certain titles."

4. **There is a general lack of professionalism.**

Sample quotes:

"We don't have a policy handbook."

"My overall impression of here is [that] there's a lot of professional courtesy that does not happen. ... Your colleague comes in and interrupts and just walks right in the middle of our conversation. ... It's kind of a little too familial, which is one of the charming things about it ... but I also think there's a kind of lack of professional etiquette."

[Re: a follow-up question about drama] "It does impact workplace culture ... just like snarky comments and stuff, but I think that's just personalities; you can't really fix that."

5. **There is a lack of clarity regarding the purpose of certain positions.**

Sample quotes:

"Everybody has kind of obscure titles and what do they, what do they really mean? How does it operate?"

"Basically, like, just people that have been here a long time that have kind of, I don't know how they came to have these fancy titles, but they're roles are not very clear, and so, is that their fault ... or was it a lack of communication?"

"You have people that are like busting their butts ... so I guess it comes down to even flow of things, but it's also because some people have been here so long they have these titles that are like insane."

6. **Some jobs are viewed as beneath certain employees.**

Sample quotes:

"Like I said previously, there is no job beneath you. I think that if you are assigned a task, you should do it. I don't think that you should be able to explain your way out of them, and I think there should be a reprimand for not doing what you're supposed to be doing."

7. **There are Significant job description overlaps.**

Sample quotes:

"It's a lack of communication, but there's also too many hands in the pot on certain things."

8. **There needs to be recognition when jobs are not being accomplished.**

Sample quotes:

[Regarding expectations] "I think [people] understand them; they just don't execute them right."

"Sometimes, I won't say every day, there are some occasions where everyone has to pick up the slack for certain people."

"If mistakes are made, some people are treated differently compared to others."

"Saying you don't know how to do something, and it's been all this time, is not a valid excuse. Learn it on YouTube."

"Yes, you're the [leader], so you should be busy, but you're running circles around your staff because your management team isn't pulling their load. ... You [the leader] shouldn't be working 80 hours a week on the most random things."

"[There are many times when] tasks don't get done without several prompts and there's always an excuse as to why it wasn't done."

9. **Communication is inconsistent and confusing.**

   Sample quotes:

   "When it comes to management, I think we lack communication. ... Some things can be compromised. There's no direct answer when it comes to staffing concerns or changes."

   [Re: what could solve communication issues] "Probably more meetings, and I don't really have time for more meetings."

   [Re: what changes you would make] "I just think communicating more and delegating better and just reprimanding the people that aren't doing their stuff."

REPRESENTED POSITIVE THEMES

1. **There is a sense of loyalty to and deep appreciation for the leader.**

   Sample quotes:

   "He [the leader] has been more open about the budget and helping me. He's been very supportive about everything."

   "He's such a good [leader] because he's got that passionate loyalty and that belief."

2. **Interviewees enjoy the overall atmosphere and enjoy their coworkers.**

   Sample quotes:

   "For the most part, you know, we have a great team."

   "I know people get frustrated with each other, at times, but it's never been … I don't know, I mean, I've been in some pretty toxic work environments, and this is not one of them."

   "I enjoy being here; this is actually the best job that I've ever had in my entire life."

3. **There is an inspirational mission communicated by the leader.**

   Sample quotes:

   "No, he's awesome as a boss; he's a dreamer and I appreciate that. [We] need a dreamer."

MISCELLANEOUS QUOTES

"Nothing will change; like I keep telling you, nothing will change."

"Just be truthful. We're all adults here; we can handle it."

"He [the leader] has an open-door policy, but he has to tell people to follow the chain of command."

"He [the leader] can get very excited and want to do everything you want to do. ... It makes us all excited but sometimes it's like, okay, chill out. When something needs to be done, it's like it [has to happen right now] whereas most of the time I don't think it should happen right now. So I think sometimes that adds to workplace stress."

"Imagine how he [the leader] could operate if he wasn't answering all these questions."

"I would love to see more diversity in who we hire."

"I think it comes down to setting clear expectations and providing the training."

[Re: the current cultural feel/morale] "I wouldn't say it's a hot mess, but yeah, sometimes it is."

"Some staff ... will not even approach certain people."

REFERENCES ─────────────────────────────

Alazani, A. S. (2018). Critical incident analysis technique to examine the issues faced by the individuals with learning disabilities. *World Journal of Education, 8,* 17–23. doi:10.5430/wje.v8n5p17

Altschuld, J. W., & Watkins, R. (2014). A primer on needs assessment: More than 40 years of research and practice. *New Directions for Evaluation, 144,* 5–18. https://doi.org/10.1002/ev.20099

Arghode, V., Jandu, N., & McLean, G. N. (2020). Exploring the connection between organizations and organisms in dealing with change. *European Journal of Training and Development, 45*(4–5), 366–380. https://doi.org/10.1108/EJTD-06-2020-0095

Barney, J. (1986). Organizational culture: Can it be a source of sustained competitive advantage? *Academy of Management, 11*(3), 656–665. https://doi.org/10.2307/258317

Beebe, S. A. (2019). Best practices of training instructional design: The needs-centered training model. In J. D. Wallace & D. Becker (Eds.), *The handbook of communication training: A best practices framework for assessing and developing competence* (pp. 254–269). Routledge.

Beebe, S. A., Mottet, T. P., & Roach, K. D. (2013). *Training and development: Communicating for success* (2nd ed.). Pearson.

Bellman, G. M. (1990). *The consultant's calling: Bringing who you are to what you do.* Jossey-Bass.

Block, P. (2011). *Flawless consulting: A guide to getting your expertise used* (3rd ed.). Jossey-Bass.

Bloom, B. (1956). *Taxonomy of educational objectives: Handbook I. Cognitive domain.* McKay.

Bollier, D. (2010). *The promise and peril of big data.* The Aspen Institute.

Braddy, P., Meade, A., & Kroustalis, C. (2006). Organizational recruitment website effects on viewers' perceptions of organizational culture. *Journal of Business and Psychology, 20*(4), 525–543. https://doi.org/10/1007/s10869-0059003-4

Clampitt, P. G. (2000). The questionnaire approach. In O. Hargie & D. Tourist (Eds.), *Handbook of communication audits for organizations* (pp. 45–65). Routledge.

Clampitt, P. G., & Downs, C. W. Employee perceptions of the relationship between communication and productivity: A field study. *The Journal of Business Communication,* 30(1), 5–29. https://doi.org/10.1177/0021943693030000101

Czarniawska, B., & Mazza, C. (2003). Consulting as a liminal space. *Human Relations, 56*(3), 267–290. https://doi.org/10.1177/0018726703056003612

Deal, T., & Kennedy, A. (1982). *Corporate culture.* Addison-Wesley.

Dickson, D. (2000). The focus group approach. In O. Hargie & D. Tourist (Eds.), *Handbook of communication audits for organizations* (pp. 85–103). Routledge.

Downs, C. W., & Adrian, A. D. (2004). *Assessing organizational communication: Strategic communication audits.* The Guilford Press.

Downs, C., & Haven, M. D. (1977). A factor analytic study of communication satisfaction. *Journal of Business Communication, 14*(3), 63–73. https://doi.org/10.1177/002194367701400306

Eriksson, P., & Kovalainen, A. (2008). *Qualitative methods in business research.* SAGE.

Frei, S., & Beebe, S. A. (2019). The communication skills of an effective trainer. In J. D. Wallace & D. Becker (Eds.), *The handbook of communication training: A best practices framework for assessing and developing competence* (pp. 348–361). Routledge.

Goldhaber, G. (1976). *The ICA communication audit: Rationale and development* [Paper presentation]. Academy of Management Convention, Kansas City, KS, United States.

Hamilton, S. (1987). *A communication audit handbook: Helping organizations communicate.* Longman.

Hayes, A. F., Slater, M. D., & Snyder, L. B. (2008). Communication network analysis. In T. Valente (Ed.), *The SAGE handbook of advanced data analysis methods for communication research* (pp. 247–273). SAGE. https://dx.doi.org/10.4135/9781452272054.n9

Hickman, A., & Pendall, R. (2018). *The end of the traditional manager.* Gallup. https://www.gallup.com/workplace/235811/end-traditional-manager.aspx

Jaff, T. (2015). Creating powerful internal communication messages. *StaffBase*. https://staffbase.com/blog/internal-communication-messages/

Kang, M., & Sung, M. (2017). How symmetrical employee communication leads to employee engagement and positive employee communication behaviors: The mediation of employee-organization relationships. *Journal of Communication Management, 21*(1), 82–102. https://doi.org/10.1108/JCOM-04-2016-0026

Karanges, E., Johnston, K., Beatson, A., & Lings, I. (2015). The influence of internal communication on employee engagement: A pilot study. *Public Relations Review, 41*(1), 129–131. https://doi.org/10.1016/j.pubrev.2014.12.003

Kaufman, R., & Guerra-Lopez, I. (2013). *Needs assessment for organizational success.* American Society for Training and Development. ASTD Press.

Kenton, B., & Moody, D. (2003). *The role of the internal consultant.* Roffey Park Institute.

Krafcik, J. F. (1988). Triumph of the lean production system. *Sloan Management Review, 30*(1), 41–52. https://search.proquest.com/docview/224963951?accountid=10003

Lynkova, D. (2021, November 1). The surprising reality of how many emails are sent per day in 2021. *Techjury.* https://techjury.net/blog/how-many-emails-are-sent-per-day/#gref

McGregor, D. (1960). *The human side of enterprise.* McGraw-Hill.

Millar, R., & Gallagher, M. (2000). The interview approach. In O. Hargie & D. Tourist (Eds.), *Handbook of communication audits for organizations* (pp. 66–84). Routledge.

Miscenko, D., & Day, D. V. (2015). Identity and identification at work. *Organizational Psychology Review, 6*(3), 215–247. https://doi.org/10.1177%2F2041386615584009

Morgan, D. (1997). *Focus groups and qualitative research* (2nd ed.). SAGE.

Newberry, C. (2021, January 6). 44 Instagram statistics that matter to marketers in 2021. *Hootsuite.* https://blog.hootsuite.com/instagram-statistics/

Reay, T., Zilber, T. B., Langley, A., & Tsoukas, H. (2019). *Institutions and organizations: A process view.* Oxford University Press. https://www.oxfordscholarship.com/view/10.1093/oso/9780198843818.001.0001/oso-9780198843818-chapter-1

Roberts, K. H., & O'Reilly, C. A. (1973). Measuring organizational communication. *Journal of Applied Psychology, 59*(3), 321–326. https://doi.org/10.1037/h0036660

Roberson, Q. M. (2006). Disentangling the meanings of diversity and inclusion in organizations. *Group & Organization Management, 31*(2), 212–236. https://doi.org/10.1177/1059601104273064

Sanchez, P. (2011). Organizational culture. In T. Gillis (Ed.). *The IABC handbook of organizational communication* (pp. 28–40). Jossey-Bass.

Sayce, D. (2020). *The number of tweets per day in 2020*. David Sayce. https://www.dsayce.com/social-media/tweets-day/

Schein, E. (2010). *Organizational culture and leadership* (4th ed.). Jossey-Bass.

Serrat, O. (2017). *Knowledge solutions*. Springer. https://doi.org/10.1007/978-981-10-0983-9_123

Sheridan, J. (1992). Organizational culture and employee retention. *Academy of Management Journal, 35*(5), 1036–1056. https://doi.org/10.2307/256539

Simpson, J. (2017, August 25). Finding brand success in the digital world. *Forbes.* https://www.forbes.com/sites/forbesagencycouncil/2017/08/25/finding-brand-success-in-the-digital-world/?sh=58b67de1626e

Stait, N. (1972). Management training and the smaller company: SWOT analysis. *Industrial and Organizational Training, 4*(7), 325–330. https://doi.org/10.1108/eb003232

Strawser, M. G., Smith, S. A., & Rubenking, B. (2021). *Multigenerational communication in organizations: Insights from the workplace*. Routledge.

Tobey, D. (2005). *Needs assessment basics*. ASTD Press.

Umphress, E., Bingham, J., & Mitchell, M. (2010). Unethical behavior in the name of the company: The moderating effect of organizational identification and positive reciprocity beliefs on unethical pro-organizational behavior. *Journal of Applied Psychology, 95*(4), 769–780. https://doi.org/10.1037/a0019214

von Platen, S. (2015). The communication consultant: An important translator for communication management. *Journal of Communication Management, 19*(2), 150–166. https://doi.org/10.1108/JCOM-06-2013-0049

Waldeck, J. H., Kearney, P., & Plax, T. (2012). *Business and professional communication in the digital age*. Cengage Learning.

Wallace, J. D., & Becker, D. (2019). *The handbook of communication training: A best practices framework for assessing and developing competence*. Routledge.

Welch, M., & Jackson, P. R. (2007). Rethinking internal communication: A stakeholder approach. *Corporate Communications: An International Journal, 12*(2), 177–198. https://doi.org/10.1108/13563280710744847

Wiio, O. A. (1975). *Systems of information, communication, and organization*. Helsinki Research Institute for Business Economics.

Witkin, B. R. (1984). *Assessing needs in educational and social programs: Using information to make decisions, set priorities, and allocate resources*. Jossey-Bass.

INDEX ―――――――――――――――――――

www.ingramcontent.com/pod-product-compliance
Lightning Source LLC
Chambersburg PA
CBHW080521220326
41599CB00032B/6159